Powering Up

Powering Up:

How Public Managers Can Take Control of Information Technology

Katherine Barrett

Richard Greene

CQ PRESS

A Division of Congressional Quarterly Inc.
Washington, D.C.

CQ Press
A Division of Congressional Quarterly Inc.
1414 22nd Street, N.W.
Washington, D.C. 20037

(202) 822-1475; (800) 638-1710
www.cqpress.com

Book design: Naylor Design, Inc.
Printed and bound in the United States of America.

04 03 02 01 00   5 4 3 2 1

The paper used in this publication meets the minimum requirements of the American National Standard for Information Sciences—Permanence of Paper for Printed Library Materials.

Library of Congress Cataloging-in-Publication Data

Barrett, Katherine.
    Powering up : how public managers can take control of
information technology / Katherine Barrett, Richard Greene.
        p.   cm.
    Includes index.
    ISBN 1-56802-575-0
    1. Public administration—Data processing.   2. Administrative
agencies—Data processing.   3. Information resources management.   4.
Information technology—Management.   I. Greene, Richard.   II. Title.

JF1525.A8 G74 2001
352.3'8213—dc21   00-064224

To the memory of Burt Greene

Contents

Foreword

Management really matters. Perhaps now, in this new economy, it matters more than ever. It especially matters at the state and local government level because that's where so many programs, including those funded by the federal government, actually are administered.

The emphasis in contemporary America is no longer on an ambitious agenda of social activism, but on how well dollars are spent and on how existing programs perform. The political imperative is to do public work well—better, faster, and cheaper, with a keen eye on what's actually achieved rather than what you're putting into it.

That's why we have committed so much time, effort, and resources to a project to gauge just how well our larger state and local governments are managing. A few years ago, thanks to the creativity and generosity of the Pew Charitable Trusts in Philadelphia, *Governing* magazine teamed up with the Maxwell School of Citizenship and Public Affairs at Syracuse University to form the Government Performance Project, an ambitious four-year program to examine how well the fifty states and larger cities and counties manage their money, their people, their infrastructure, and their information technology, and how well they manage for results.

So far, this academic-journalistic partnership has published two reports, assigning grades in each of the five areas studied for all the states and the thirty-five largest cities. Another report on the states will be published in early 2001, and one on the largest counties will appear in early 2002. The first two reports attracted extensive press coverage across the nation, which in turn helped motivate many states and cities by drawing attention to and improving their effort. That was exactly the intended effect.

What have we learned? In a word, plenty. So much, in fact, that we are publishing our findings in a series of books authored by the academics and journalists deeply involved with the project. This one, *Powering Up*, by *Governing* project editors Katherine Barrett and Richard Greene, is the first in the series. It covers what we've learned about how governments are managing information technology (IT). We started here, because it has become clear that IT is fundamentally important to managing everything else. More books are coming. The next is Sally Coleman Selden's book on human resource management. Another one is planned on managing for results.

These books are aimed at everyone interested in how we're managing our states and localities, from governors, mayors, and their appointees to career managers, consultants, academics, and their students—the managers of tomorrow. These books are intended to be accessible, useful, and interesting and to further share the wealth of information gathered in the Government Performance Project. We believe that the books will demonstrate the wide range of creativity and innovation that is present in state and local governments and make the point once again that management is not boring: it is critical to good government.

Peter Harkness
Editor and Publisher
Governing

Patricia W. Ingraham
Director, Government Performance Project
Distinguished Professor, Maxwell School of Citizenship and Public Affairs, Syracuse University

Preface

In recent years, public sector managers have become increasingly dependent on information technology (IT) to do their jobs well. In fact, superior management of most other governmental systems—including finance, human resources, and capital allocation—is now nearly impossible without proper use of computer and communication systems.

At the same time, with the exception of those managers whose jobs are focused exclusively on technology, many in government have neither the desire nor the need to understand the seemingly inscrutable functionings of the high-tech equipment that makes up an IT system. Yet these managers' jobs often require that they make decisions regarding that technology or oversee the decisions of others who work with it.

The parallel here to the airline industry is strong. In the earliest days of commercial aviation, many of the major airlines were founded and run by one-time pilots. Today, no one would assume that the ability to fly a jetliner is critical to managing an airline. The body of knowledge that high-level airline managers require is different—and their most important connection to actually flying the aircraft is understanding how to hire, train, and retain qualified pilots. The same is true in IT. In the past, the men and women who made most high-level decisions about IT in the public sector were technologists themselves. Those days have passed.

Why is management of IT in the public sector important? The most obvious reason is that billions of taxpayer dollars are being spent each year on all manner of technology in cities and states, from desktop computers to mainframes. The wisdom with which those dollars are spent varies wildly, but it's clear that a link can be drawn between good management and sensible resource allocation.

As Patricia Ingraham and Philip Joyce wrote in a paper titled, "Government Management: Defining and Assessing Performance": "We believe (as do many public management scholars and government managers) that a well-managed government (or government program or agency) all other things being equal, delivers greater value for public money than a poorly managed one."

Yet despite the overwhelming importance of IT in the public sector, no books previously published have straightforwardly set forth essential principles of IT management within government entities. A number of good books—some scholarly, some more popular in nature—have been written for private sector corporations. But attempts to extend the lessons of private corporations to the public sector are fraught with peril.

With that thought in mind, we offer this volume, which attempts to provide a basic guide for public sector managers—and students who are learning to fill those jobs—about IT management. It has purposefully been written in a way that avoids jargon and puts a high priority on easy comprehension of sometimes complex issues. Each chapter ends with a series of "In Summary" points, to highlight the most significant concepts explored. The authors believe that readers will profit from the book even if they have little background on the nitty-gritty aspects of technology.

In addition, *Powering Up: How Public Managers Can Take Control of Information Technology* is not an academic text in the true sense of that word; the conclusions reached are based not on the academic literature but on the experiences of real-world practitioners in all fifty states and the nations' thirty-five largest cities (a list of which is found in Appendix B, starting on page 178). The readers who will find it most useful are those in search of lessons gained from experience and not scholarly advice.

The book has four essential goals:

To provide readers with a broad overview of the state of the art of IT management in the fifty states and the nation's largest cities.

To highlight successful practices in the states and cities so that students may learn from them and practitioners may emulate them.

To highlight failed practices in the cities and states so that students and practitioners may learn to avoid them.

To use a journalistic approach that sets forth the principles of good IT management in a way that is not only informative but also fun to read.

The vast majority of the information in *Powering Up* comes from the Government Performance Project (GPP), a joint venture between the Maxwell School of Citizenship and Public Affairs at Syracuse University and *Governing* magazine, funded by the Pew Charitable Trusts. During the past several years, the GPP thoroughly analyzed management practices in the nation's fifty states and thirty-five largest cities. Results have been published in *Governing* and analyzed in academic papers. But an enormous amount of scholarly work remains to be done; and one issue of *Governing* barely scratches the surface of all the information garnered from the project. This book draws on all the practical lessons the authors learned about IT management in putting together these reports.

Organization of the Book

The introduction to *Powering Up* contains a detailed explanation of the methodology used in the GPP itself. The next couple of chapters set the stage for an understanding of IT in the public sector: the benefits of good management, the pitfalls of bad, and the risks in assuming an approach that depends exclusively on so-called "best practices." The following two chapters delve into the structure of IT management in cities and states, as well as the proper roles of chief information officers and other IT leaders. The next seven chapters—the core of the book—focus on the basic management principles explored via the GPP's criteria. These chapters give readers a basic understanding of the current practices being followed—as well as some of those that have proved successful—in the following areas:

Project management
Strategic planning
Procurement
Outsourcing
Training end-users and IT specialists
Cost-benefit analysis
Appropriate public sector use of the Internet

In addition, three chapter-length case studies focus on the cities of Philadelphia and Phoenix and on the state of Washington. Even though every chapter includes a number of examples, these case studies should be useful for readers—both practitioners and students—who wish to see how the principles set forth have been applied in a broader context and how they fit together in a single major IT project. The Philadelphia chapter focuses on the city's efforts to implement a Geographic Information System; the Phoenix chapter explores the city's implementation of a new financial management system; and the Washington chapter examines that state's effort to allow businesses to file their taxes electronically.

Following the main text are four appendixes, two of which provide reprints of the actual GPP report, as published in the pages of *Governing*. These appendixes are by no means complete reports about the eighty-five jurisdictions covered. Instead, they are provided to permit readers to make quick comparisons between individual cities and states. The book concludes with a glossary of IT terminology and an index.

Acknowledgments

The most important people to acknowledge are the men and women who gave many hours of their time completing lengthy survey instruments and then more hours being interviewed. These people are listed in Appendix A, starting on page 175.

Of course, thanks are due to the Pew Charitable Trusts, without whose sponsorship the GPP—and this book—would not have been possible.

Others who should be noted for their aid include Patricia Ingraham, Syracuse University Professorship of Distinction, professor of public administration and director of the Government Performance Project during its first three years; Philip Joyce, formerly of Syracuse and now of George Washington University, who managed the academic side of the GPP in its first two years; B. J. Reed, head of the department of public administration at the University of Nebraska, Omaha, who spearheads the academic side of the GPP's current IT research; Amy Schmit and Anthony Stacy, project managers who provided invaluable organizational skills; Amy Kneedler, now assistant professor of political science at the University of Connecticut, who patiently worked to adjust and improve the actual survey instrument; and a squadron of graduate students, who pored over sky-high stacks of documents.

The information derived by the GPP was based essentially on the experiences of practitioners. So, in an effort to ensure that *Powering Up* is useful to an academic audience as well, the proposal and text of the book have been carefully evaluated by a panel of academics including Mary Maureen Brown, of the University of North Carolina, Charlotte; N. Joseph Cayer, of Arizona State University; Louise Comfort, of the University of Pittsburgh; Jon Gant, of Indiana University; Dahlia Bradshaw Lynn, of the University of Southern Maine; and James Thompson, of the University of Illinois, Chicago.

The topics covered in this book are fundamentally linked to the criteria used in the GPP to evaluate cities and states. Those criteria were developed in large part by an expert advisory panel that included John Carrow, chief information officer and vice president of corporate information technology at Unisys Corp.; John Kost, senior vice president at Federal Sources Inc.; David McClure, senior assistant director at the U.S. General Accounting Office; Jerry Mechling, director of strategic computing and telecommunications in the public sector at the John F. Kennedy School of Government, Harvard University; Jasmeet Seehra, policy analyst in the Office of

Information and Regulatory Affairs of the Office of Management and
Budget, in Washington, D.C.; Peter Harkness, editor and publisher
of *Governing*; and Philip Joyce.

On the journalistic side, thanks are due to many on the *Governing*
staff who made this effort possible, including Alan Ehrenhalt, Elder
Witt, Anne Jordan, John Martin, and Ellen Perlman. Of special note
is Peter Harkness, our publisher, whose drive and determination
made the GPP and this book a reality. Thanks also, to our fact-
checker, Mark Wellborn.

We appreciate the input of various private sector leaders who
graciously answered our Internet query about information technology. Bob Campbell, of Deloitte Consulting, in Austin, deserves
special mention here for his invaluable insights about procurement.

Finally, a debt of gratitude is owed to Charisse Kiino, our editor
at CQ Press. She stands out for proving that kindness and understanding can coexist with intellect. We also extend our thanks to
others at CQ Press: manuscript editor Jon Preimesberger, indexer
Kim Johnson, and proofreader Barbara Johnson. As always, we
appreciate the work of our agent, Stuart Krichevsky, who protects
us even when we don't think we need to be protected. And, last, our
appreciation goes to our children, Ben and Sandy, who like
computers but are thoroughly sick and tired of hearing us talk about
information technology.

Introduction: What This Book Is—and Is Not

Before you read even a single paragraph in the pages that follow, three important disclosures are essential.

Disclosure number one: the authors of this book are journalists. Not academics. Not technologists. Rather, traditional ink-stained wretches who gather their information primarily by talking to people—lots of people. As you'll see, this is a rather rare journalistic effort, in that it was conducted hand in hand with a troop of academics. But, ultimately, the approach that prevails in the pages that follow is that of reporters who try to learn from the best sources available and communicate the lessons learned in the most straightforward way.

Thus, if you're expecting a traditional academic textbook, which relies fundamentally on theory and university-related literature, then you've got the wrong book. Similarly, if you're hoping for information that will help you to design an efficient network of desktop computers, you're also in the wrong place.

On the other hand, if you are a nontechnologically oriented student of public administration or a public sector manager interested in finding out what's happening in information technology management in the real world—with a solid notion of techniques that work and that don't work—welcome. Similarly, if you are a technology specialist who wants to understand how to manage your specialty—in areas such as strategic planning, procurement, and training—stick around, too.

Disclosure number two: one of the goals in writing this book has been to provide the most up-to-date information available. Still, given the speed of change in information technology (IT), some of the anecdotal information contained here is already out of date. In fact, with IT, anything you hear on a Monday morning may be out of date by Wednesday afternoon. But even if the cities or states described have already changed in significant ways, the lessons learned from their experiences during the past couple of years are still very much worthwhile. What's more, subsequent editions will ensure that *Powering Up* keeps up with the evolving nature of the subject covered.

Disclosure number three: given the nature of the research that provides the underpinnings for this book (and much more about that in a moment), the definition of information technology used here is very broad. Essentially, it covers any system used by governments to facilitate the creation and flow of information. Of course, the emphasis tends to be somewhat more on cutting-edge technology. To be sure, telephones are an integral part of IT systems, but you will find very little material about telecommunications in this book. The examples we give generally tend to focus on four essential areas:

◆ Entity-wide computer systems, such as those used for human resources or payroll.
◆ Agency-specific systems, such as imaging equipment used to help a department of motor vehicles maintain its driver's license files.
◆ Commodity-type items, such as desktop computers, which are used throughout government.
◆ Computer networks used to tie together all of the above.

The Government Performance Project

The vast majority of the information contained in the pages that follow emanates from the Government Performance Project (GPP). This effort began in 1996 with funding from the Pew Charitable Trusts. The GPP is an effort to rate the management performance of state and local governments around the United States through a process that involves the skills of both journalists at *Gov-*

erning and academics at the Maxwell School of Citizenship and Public Affairs at Syracuse University and other institutions, notably the University of Nebraska in Omaha.

Unlike other popular efforts to evaluate cities, this project has nothing to do with quality of life. Not a single government is evaluated on the basis of the climate in its area or the proximity to airports. In fact, the city awarded the highest grades—Phoenix—has a notably weak public transportation system. Instead, the GPP focuses on the nitty-gritty government management that underlies all successful programs. Five areas of government management were selected upon which to focus. These included financial management, human resources, capital management, managing for results, and—most important from the point of view of this book—information technology.

As you might expect, the starting place for the project was determining what criteria to use in evaluating management in a city or state information technology system. The process began with long discussions among public administration experts at the Maxwell School, who reviewed the available academic literature on information technology management. Then, an expert advisory panel (whose members are named in the preface) was convened.

Over the course of several sessions, this panel developed broad criteria for the GPP that were then tested out in a year-long pilot project involving four cities, four states, and two counties.

In the second year of the project, the criteria were revisited and slightly refined by a panel that included members of the *Governing* staff as well as Patricia Ingraham, director of the Alan K. Campbell Institute at the Maxwell School; Amy Kneedler, now assistant professor of political science at the University of Connecticut, and B. J. Reed, chair of the Public Administration Department at the University of Nebraska in Omaha. Through the remainder of that year, Reed continued to oversee the academic side of the IT portion of the initiative.

In February 1999 *Governing* published the first GPP report in what is hoped to be an annual series. The first report dealt with the states. In February 2000, the second installment, focusing on the nation's thirty-five largest cities, was published.

The GPP Criteria

In the GPP segment that examined IT management, the first of the eight basic criteria focused on the actual utility of IT in the government workplace. This meant evaluating whether IT systems provided information that supported managers' needs and strategic goals. Special emphasis was placed on very large agency systems and entity-wide systems for financial management, human resources, and capital management.

Another criteria focused on the entity's use of the Internet to communicate internally with government workers and externally with citizens and other stakeholders. A survey instrument was designed that helped graduate students at the Maxwell School review Web sites in a systematic way to determine how thoroughly they informed users about the enterprise as a whole as well as its agencies. In addition, the Web sites were examined to see if they solicited input from stakeholders, allowed for transactions (like purchasing licenses or paying parking tickets), and were easily navigated.

The remaining six criteria were more clearly rooted in management systems that influenced the skill and efficiency with which IT dollars are spent and IT systems are implemented and utilized. Put in question form, they are as follows:

1. Does the city or state have a coherent architecture for information technology systems?

   - Does the entity have standards in place for information technology, or a general architecture that ensures compatibility?
   - Are there any areas for which standards are still missing?
   - Are the standards well enforced?
   - Are there many stand-alone systems still in use?
   - Are there any agencies that are not required to comply with city or statewide standards (for example, the police department)? If this is the case, are these agencies' lack of compliance an obstacle to the free flow of information?
   - Does the city or state have one e-mail system, with easy transfer of documents via attachments?

2. Is there meaningful, multiyear information technology planning?

   ◆ Does the entity have a formal IT strategic plan?
   ◆ Do agencies have their own formal IT strategic plans?
   ◆ Do these strategic plans include the following: a vision statement; goals and objectives; measures of the progress toward those goals and objectives; discussion of potential obstacles?
   ◆ Does the strategic plan tie these various elements together, so users of the plan can understand how very specific objectives fit in with the broad vision?
   ◆ Is the strategic plan a genuinely useful document—that is, are people actually using it?
   ◆ Is the strategic plan used in allocating resources?
   ◆ Is the strategic plan updated (though not necessarily rewritten) on a regular basis; at least once a year?
   ◆ Do IT strategic plans tie into and reflect the goals in other entity-wide business plans?

3. Does the structure of IT management effectively balance central controls and agency flexibility?

   ◆ Does the central office ensure that standards are being followed?
   ◆ Does the central office have the capacity to halt projects in agencies that are failing?
   ◆ Does the central office have sufficient information to ensure there are no redundant systems being purchased in the agencies?
   ◆ Is the central office headed by an individual who is fundamentally responsible for strategy and planning; not day-to-day problems?
   ◆ Is the head of the central office placed high enough in the government structure to ensure that IT has a significant place in decision making?
   ◆ Do agencies have enough flexibility to seek out specific solutions for their individual problems?

- Are agencies consulted in entity-wide decisions? Do they genuinely feel involved in the process of making IT decisions that affect them?

4. Is information technology training adequate for end-users and information technology specialists?

   - Does the central office have a solid idea of how much training is actually being offered in the agencies?
   - Do the majority of end-users receive sufficient training in the software and hardware they are using to use it efficiently?
   - Do IT specialists receive sufficient training?
   - Are creative means being used to provide training where traditional classrooms are not effective (for example, on-line training)?
   - Beyond sufficient training being available, do managers encourage employees to take advantage of it?
   - Are there incentives for individuals to become better trained?

5. Does the city or state have the capacity to evaluate the extent to which benefits of an information technology system justified the investment?

   - When an agency requests an IT investment, is the agency required to present a complete business case, indicating all costs and both monetary and nonmonetary benefits?
   - If an agency doesn't present a complete business case, to what extent is it required to justify the investment? Is the justification adequate to make reasoned decisions?
   - After an IT investment has been approved and implemented, does the city or state make certain that promised benefits have been delivered?
   - If promised benefits have not been delivered, are actions of some kind taken (for example, are further requests from that agency scrutinized more thoroughly?)

6. Is procurement of needed technology conducted in a timely manner, both for commodity-type items and those that are more complex?

- Are master contracts used for the majority of commodity-type items (such as desktop computers or network routers)?
- Are the number of master contracts kept within control?
- Are other governmental entities included in the master contracts, in order to get better prices for larger purchases?
- Do agencies feel that it takes overly long from the date work on a request for proposal (RFP) is begun, until the actual technology is delivered?
- Are RFPs generally done adequately the first time they are written; or do they frequently have to be rewritten?
- Are RFPs sufficiently flexible to allow for the creative input of the vendors?

With the above criteria in hand, how precisely is the annual GPP conducted? The methodology has evolved over the course of the past several years and continues to change over time. But essentially it is a bifurcated process, with a journalistic team at *Governing* magazine approaching it from one perspective, and an academic team approaching it from another. Here's how that works.

Step one is to design and disseminate a lengthy survey instrument. The vast majority of the entities covered generally complete the entire survey (in fact, only one state and one city refused to cooperate with the GPP in any way in its first two years). In addition to the actual instrument, large quantities of documents are either provided by the entities or procured by the GPP staff. With all that material in hand, both journalists and academics can begin their work; approaching the same material in somewhat different ways.

The Academic Approach

Journalists tend to think academics focus too heavily on methodology and theory. Academics think journalists do not report on public management to any great depth. In reality, the GPP project demonstrates each may underestimate the other.

The academic portion of the GPP does follow a rigorous process to ensure quality, consistency, and equity in the assessment and assignment of grades for cities and states. Academics also recognize, however, that to be useful, research needs to be responsive and understandable to practitioners and academics alike.

The initial step in compiling the IT segment of the GPP survey is to assemble an IT team with a faculty advisor to oversee the process. The IT team is one of several working on different segments of the project. These teams, with graduate student help, work under the direction of the director of the Campbell Institute at Maxwell and the GPP project manager. Any faculty member knows that quality graduate students can make or break good research because they are often the ones left to carry out the day-to-day analysis. Such is the case in working on the IT segment where students spend endless hours reviewing surveys and documents for the project.

After the Maxwell School assembles the faculty advisor and graduate students on each segment of the GPP, the real work begins. The assessment criteria for IT that was mentioned earlier are the key building blocks for the IT team in developing its evaluation. Care is taken that the IT survey is constructed in such a way that cities and states are assessed only on the criteria identified, and not on other factors. The criteria provide direction to the faculty and staff in developing the IT survey instrument. This survey is designed to achieve several goals:

1. To match the criteria. This ensures that data used to rank participants is appropriate.
2. To be clear and precise so that responses are consistent across states and communities. The ability to compare responses is necessary to ensure rankings are not arbitrarily assigned as a result of different interpretations of the survey.
3. To be appropriate to the ability and capacity of states and communities to respond. The more data and information requested, the less likely those responding are willing and able to provide a quality response. While certain information is helpful to have, it is often not critical to the assessment process. For this reason the

survey must only address those items central to ranking states and communities' management capacity in IT.

Along with completing the survey, cities and states are asked to provide supporting documentation that helps clarify and expand on their survey responses. Some cities and states provide limited information. Others produce volumes of papers, reports, and other documents.

Once the surveys are returned, the tough part of the academic process begins. The academic team must make sure it can compare responses across cities or states. This is where coding comes into play. The survey asks for specific information about such things as IT training, architecture, citizen participation, and procurement. To evaluate the responses fairly, each survey response needs to be reviewed the same way using the same criteria. For example, one question asks about the IT planning process. This question needs to be coded so that every survey response is assessed the same way. First, the question needs to be coded as follows:

1. Yes, they have a technology plan.
2. No, they don't have a technology plan.
3. No, but they are working to develop a technology plan.

Those having plans are ranked more highly than those who don't. Those who have technology plans underway are ranked more highly then those who have no plan to plan.

Next, the responses are coded to identify components included in the technology plan. Not all technology plans are equal in terms of quality or comprehensiveness. The faculty advisor provides a listing of common elements for such plans and then the city's responses are matched to these elements. Documentation becomes important here. Cities and states may not put information in the survey, but they may send their IT plan along with other documents. This requires the IT team members to go to the original documents to get the required information.

Coding is difficult under any circumstances. It is even more difficult when questions are open-ended. Some cities and states go into great depth in answering questions while others give short one- or two-sentence responses. The key is not to rate cities and states on what they don't report, but rather on what they do report. For this reason, coding must depend on the documents as well as the surveys. This is also where the journalists come in because they often can add information from the interviews that does not exist in either the survey responses or the documentation.

Another important issue in coding is to make sure the reviewers are consistent. One action taken by the Maxwell team is to go through a set of survey responses and then go back and look at the first surveys coded to make sure the process is the same across all cities and states. The tendency is to be more harsh in coding early in the process. This review ensures that all the responses are assessed fairly. It is also useful to have someone else review what has been coded to see if the evaluations are similar.

The students assisting on the academic team have the primary responsibility for coding and verification of information. The IT team divides the work so that each student has responsibility for certain elements of the IT survey. The survey itself is divided into categories for coding that coincide with the criteria mentioned above.

Once all the surveys are coded, the faculty advisor and students sit down together and go through the responses from each government entity and confirm each coding rank. An overall rating is then given to each city and state. Some categories are given more weight than others. For example, architecture and managerial support are valued more highly than training or procurement. Also, these sessions allow the IT team to determine internal consistencies and linkages between different components. How is the cost-benefit analysis component linked to planning or to procurement components? Are citizens involved in the IT planning process? How is managerial support linked to quality and integration of architecture? The results are a final academic grade for each city or state.

The Journalistic Approach

No matter how carefully a survey instrument is designed, and no matter how many documents are carefully reviewed, there is simply no substitute for actual human contact to help put information into context and to filter out inaccuracies. This is where the *Governing* staff, with its direct contact with people both inside and outside each of the government entities, participates in the GPP.

Step one for the *Governing* staff is to review carefully the survey instruments submitted by the city or state, to see how an entity describes its own systems. Along with information and analysis of the surveys and significant documents that flow in from the Maxwell School, journalists prepare lengthy lists of follow-up questions to ask selected individuals at each entity.

In every case, the entity was free to choose the individual or individuals within their government with whom interviews were conducted. The vast majority selected a chief information officer (CIO) or the equivalent; in other cases a deputy in that department was chosen. Frequently, budget office or administrative officials were also present at the interview. In all, approximately 100 people were interviewed about information technology; and their experiences, judgments, and commentary provide the basis of much of the book that follows.

At the same time, interviews were being conducted with officials who were involved in the remaining four segments of the GPP—financial, personnel, capital, and managing for results. In all segments, officials were queried about their use of information technology. This allowed for a potent cross-reference for the information being provided by CIOs. For example, if the information officer in a city indicated that the city's personnel system was state of the art; and the personnel chief said that the city couldn't do workforce planning, because the computers didn't produce reports on a timely basis, that presented grounds for further research and questioning. Similar cross-checks were provided by interviews with auditors, outside observers of city and state government, legislative staffers, and other individuals both inside and outside government.

The primary IT interviews by *Governing* staff generally ran about two hours in length. In many cases, information provided on the survey was adjusted in these conversations for a variety of reasons: sometimes a question on the survey was simply misinterpreted; in other cases the facts had changed in the months subsequent to the survey response; in still others probing questions revealed that cities or states were painting a too-positive or too-negative self-portrait. In all instances, context was provided for both positive and negative attributes of IT systems. Some entities are deeply decentralized, for example, out of a sense that that is a superior management approach. Others follow that route because there have been decades of power battles resulting in internal fiefdoms. Although this context may or may not influence the actual rating, it provided much of the substance for this book.

Generally, additional information is faxed or e-mailed to the GPP offices to help follow up on questions that couldn't be answered during the conversation.

After the interviews are completed, *Governing* staffers then assemble the information from the survey, evaluations emanating from the Maxwell School, and the material from all the interviews onto so-called "summary sheets," which were divided by criteria. This permits a criteria-by-criteria evaluation of the entity. Unlike the academic analysis, there is no numerical distillation of the material. Although the journalistic evaluators attempt to consistently compare the quality of management across the board, obviously, there is a certain amount of subjectivity to the grading.

By the same token, the journalistic approach permits a fuzzier kind of logic than does the academic. For example, small states that are generally controlled by one political party are seen to have less of a need for a very rigorous strategic plan than larger states that have a great need for a nonpoliticized guide to future decisions. So, although the academic approach would give both states the same amount of credit for such an effort, the journalistic effort would draw a distinction between the two.

What's more, the interview approach extended the project's ability to give proper credit for "momentum," to use GPP jargon. As mentioned above, a city that is working on a technology plan got more credit from the academics than did one that had no plan and no efforts to create one. However, there is a wide spectrum of efforts to move forward, and only through rigorous interviewing (and not always then) is it possible to determine how seriously an entity is taking its efforts to improve management.

All partners in the GPP agreed from the onset that it was crucial that both the journalists and academics came to a consensus on the conclusions reached. So, at this point, with grades in hand from both partners, the final stage in the process begins.

The Journalists and Academics Meet

It has been startling—and certainly pleasant—to discover that when the journalists and academics compared grades for the first two GPP efforts, they were in tandem the vast majority of the time. Though no careful analysis has been performed to determine why this was so, this did demonstrate that both approaches had validity.

Sometimes, inevitably, there was disagreement, and at that point a criteria-by-criteria comparison between the two methods of evaluation was undertaken to determine where the disagreement came from. Reasons for disagreements varied. In the case of Seattle, for example, the academics believed the city to be better managed than did the journalists. The reason? It was discovered that the interviewees had been overly self-critical by pointing out problems in their systems that weren't even being considered in other cities. When this became clear, the interview-based grades were raised. In other instances, the academics adjusted their conclusions; often because the journalists had gathered information that was either newer than that on the survey or differed from that in the survey in a significant fashion.

By the time the conclusions were published in *Governing*, however, there was absolute agreement between both teams that the grades and text, as shown, was as accurate as possible, given the time limitations of the exercise itself.

The Published Reports

The first GPP report covered the fifty states and was published in *Governing*'s February 1999 issue. Its conclusions had a great effect on the states involved, and the actual publication was a finalist in the National Magazine Awards' public service category. The following year, the nation's thirty-five largest cities (as ranked by revenues) were analyzed; the publication appeared in February 2000.

As had always been anticipated, there were some complaints about the conclusions reached. Most significant, not one city or state took exception to the essential criteria used in information technology. (There were some complaints about criteria in other areas covered.) The fact that eighty-five entities were publicly evaluated— many of them negatively—and not one wrote to take exception to the criteria used would appear to be the best evidence possible that those ground rules were sensible and broadly acceptable.

The fruits of this effort—beyond the actual issues of *Governing*— included assembling what may well be the largest conglomeration of information about information technology in cities and states in the world.

The pages that follow are a distillation of these findings. Undoubtedly there will be consultants and academics who would arrive at different conclusions than those reported here. In an area that's as quickly developing as information technology, different points of view are inevitable.

Though the origins of the criteria were academically oriented, the findings are focused in the real world; real practitioners talking about what works and what doesn't work for them. Each and every significant point made in the chapters to come is backed up by thoughts or anecdotes provided by the practitioners themselves. Some, as you'll see, are rather feisty in attitude; others are more philosophical about the obstacles they confront daily.

Finally, the examples that follow leave open the possibility that there may be a variety of solutions to similar problems. There is no pretense here that there's some single magic key to success that will result in a flawless, fully integrated, information technology system affordable to any government. If one existed, you can be sure, every practitioner in state and local government would already know about it.

1

IT on the Front Lines

People are always comparing governments to the *Queen Mary,* or even the *Titanic*—entities that are large, cumbersome, and not easy to turn around quickly. And in a great many ways, that's a reasonable metaphor. Many city, state, and county managers like to stick to reliable, proven ways of managing; whether it's in the realm of financial management, human resources, or capital investment.

But when it comes to use of computers and communications equipment—what we'll broadly refer to as information technology (IT)—governments have been far more like speedboats than cruise ships. Just a decade ago, states simply didn't have Web sites. The first government Web sites appearing in the early 1990s were minimalist affairs compared to the multimedia shows operating today. Perhaps most telling, articles written at the time had to take pains to define the "Internet," in case nontechnical readers were lost in the jargon.

"I have a friend who is a surgeon. I read more than he does, just to keep my head above water as to what's new this week," related Courtney Harrington, deputy director of the Department of Information Technology in Honolulu. "If I look back as to where I was with my personal computer two years ago, it feels like eons."

Today, every state and major city is on-line. And numerous not so major cities are, too. Lava Hot Springs, Idaho, with 450 citizens, is hardly a bustling metropolis. It's 150 miles from the nearest large city. But all 450 residents can find out about their town by going on-line to find information about its government, recreation and attractions, businesses, and more. (You can, by the way, experience the beauty of Lava Hot Springs on a "scenic wagon ride, powered by Belgian horses or mules," according to the site.)

The fact is, in the old days (that would be any time prior to the Clinton administration in high-tech terms), government managers tried to improve service by getting employees to work harder and by trying to streamline processes. Managers are still doing these things, but more and more they look toward the magic of the microchip as well.

In fact, there's a real risk of relying too heavily on technology, by assuming that technology is the solution, whatever the problem. As Tennessee's chief information officer Bradley Dugger explained: "One of the things that we have really pushed over the years is that IT should solve a business problem for you. If it doesn't solve a business problem for you, you shouldn't have it."

This isn't to say that everyone has become dizzy with the potential of technology. There's still a hefty cadre of government employees (including even some governors and mayors) who may give lip service to the benefits of IT but, on the whole, would just as soon steer clear of any machine that beeps back at you each time you make a mistake. David Sullivan, chief information officer in Virginia Beach, related, "Last year, we didn't distribute hard-printed budgets like in the past. They're distributed on our intranet, instead. But some people complain they still want the hard copy. We say 'Go have it printed out.' The cultural thing is coming along. But it will take a while for people to be used to having everything at their fingertips instead of on a bookshelf."

Benefits of Technology

Sullivan is right, of course. But given the benefits of new technologies, the march forward is inexorable. Here are just a few examples at the state level:

◆ Massachusetts citizens long resented the time and trouble required to renew car and truck registrations, request duplicate registrations, order special plates, and pay citations. The state was the first in the country to offer these services on-line. Now secure transactions are available to millions of people, saving time and eliminating long lines at Registry of Motor Vehicles offices.

◆ Michigan agency heads were frustrated by their inability to purchase important equipment as quickly and easily as they wanted. In response the state became one of the first to implement a statewide, on-line financial accounting and purchasing system that includes all agencies in state government. Now, purchasing transactions can be conducted without leaving a computer screen. Michigan also put into place a data warehouse, through which agencies could get easy access to pertinent information concerning accounting and purchasing questions.

◆ Missourians who qualify to receive a whole range of benefits no longer have to wait for checks via mail. They now access those benefits with an electronic benefits transfer card that can be used at nearly all automatic teller machines. This card, which accesses a person's food stamp dollars much like a bank debit card, is also accepted by many grocers who participate in the food stamp program. Not only are the recipients happier, taxpayers have saved about $1 million a year over the paper-based system.

◆ Montana had been incapable of providing managers with good financial, human resource, and budgeting information, in a speedy way. In the past couple of years, it has engaged in one of the most widespread IT upgrades around, with its Statewide Accounting Budget and Human Resource System (SABHRS), a comprehensive effort to tie together all these fields. As one IT manager said, "Now we can dream up and craft a report in a day or two that would have taken months before."

And those are only states that begin with the letter M. Cities are also discovering the benefits of new technology. Philadelphia, San Jose, and New York are using Geographic Information Systems (GIS) for a nearly endless list of purposes such as fighting crime, by tracking concentrations of criminal activity, and coordinating public works efforts to ensure a street isn't paved one week and torn up the next.

Meanwhile, the Computer Aided Dispatch system in Austin, Texas, tracks emergency vehicles on a real-time basis, which allows the police department to make minute-to-minute decisions on where to deploy resources. San Francisco's new human resources system is facilitating hiring approvals in half an hour when it previously took weeks. And Philadelphia's Department of Revenue has invested more than $9.3 million for five related computer systems that have significantly improved current and delinquent tax collections, producing an estimated $100 million in additional revenues to the city through fiscal year 2000.

Pitfalls

Whatever the problem, technology appears to be part of the solution. That is, of course, unless technology is the problem!

There's a too-long list of IT disasters in which states, cities—and, of course, the federal government—have spent huge sums of money on computer systems that have accomplished little or nothing of value.

One of the more infamous incidents befell the California Department of Motor Vehicles. Beginning in 1988, the state spent more than $60 million over seven years—big bucks even for California—for a new system for driver's licenses and registration information. The initial result was about as much forward motion as a stalled car on the Santa Monica Freeway at rush hour—which is to say, none. In 1995 the state launched a new effort, but as of March 1999 the state's legislative analyst indicated she had no idea when the new system will be installed or how much it will cost—mainly because Y2K efforts that year had derailed work on it.

Nevada's new state welfare system has been missing deadlines and going over budget for about a decade now. Meanwhile, the federal government, which requires that all states have a system in place to monitor child support payments and track deadbeat dads, has been threatening the state with millions of dollars in fines.

At the city level, St. Paul spent $1.6 million on a state-of-the-art human resources system then canceled it after figuring out that the city couldn't afford to run the system once it was finished.

The truth is, however, the well-publicized problems represent just a few megabytes on the hard drive of IT shortcomings. They're well known largely because some watchdog agency gets sufficiently rankled that it issues press releases. Other problems escape attention. Many of them are far subtler than outright failures—they fly under radar for years, as they get worse and worse.

For many years, Kansas' budget office had difficulties analyzing the states finances effectively because it was working with an antique computer system (which actually had to be fixed a few years ago simply so it could use numbers bigger than one billion). Connecticut would love to be able to do workforce planning, but its human resources system can barely tell managers how many people even work for the state; much less analyze trends in hiring practices. For a while, it was heading resolutely toward privatizing its information technology, but that process seems indefinitely stalled right now. New Mexico has no computerized central inventory of capital assets—which makes it very difficult to engage in meaningful prioritization of new building projects.

Politics

Of course, government managers often have to deal with a variety of obstacles that their counterparts in the business world never have to face. For example, when the president of a Fortune 500 company discovers that a major competitor is attracting better workers with a super-sophisticated computer system that manages personnel—does he or she have to get approval of the board of directors to purchase the same system? Does the CEO have to consider whether consumers would rather the CEO spend money on painting the company's factory than buying the new computer system? Probably not. And that's why business managers are in a better position in deciding about new technology than are most government leaders.

Generally, when a city's chief information officer learns about some incredibly useful computer system, his or her first thought may well be of the number of people who have to be convinced that the system is worthwhile. There's the mayor. And members of the city council. And the city's finance officials. And even if the chief information officer convinces all these others, everyone is deeply aware that if something goes wrong with the new system, and it is reported by the newspapers, there's the real possibility that voters will be angry that money was spent on bells and whistles instead of basic government services.

Of course, this may be stating the obvious fact that government managers have to deal with a political process. But it is always important to remember that politics often slows down progress and can sometimes even stop it dead in its tracks.

When Maine, for example, needed a new computer system to support its budgeting efforts, its legislature might well have authorized the money to pay for it. However, the state's lawmakers got caught in a wrangle over whether or not Maine should be employing performance-based budgeting. And one of the things the new computer system could possibly have supported was performance-based budgeting. As a result no money was budgeted; and a budget management system remained that didn't allow agencies to develop their budgets and didn't meet analytical reporting needs of the bureau of the budget.

Political factors can be particularly pronounced in states or cities in which power is divided among a number of elected officials. In some cities, for example, the comptroller's office may have control over the financial management system—to the frustration of the budget office.

In Indianapolis, the city's former CIO Emily Duncan pointed out the potential impact of the recent election, which resulted in the first partisan split in that city in thirty-two years. "The Mayor is a Democrat and the remainder of the Information Technology Council are Republicans. And as a result, I think this position is going to get to be more politicized. It's going to be a tougher role."

Money and Management

Of course, politics is a reality in every city and state in the country. So, what's the difference between states that are leading the pack in their use of information technology and those that are baying at the moon? It really boils down to two words: money and management.

The first of the two can be dispensed with in two par
The second is the subject of the remainder of this book.

The sad truth is, if a city or state doesn't have the money to spend on information technology, it isn't going to reap much benefit from recent advances in the field. The same is true of entities that have the money but don't want to spend it in this way. Information technology can be prohibitively expensive for many entities in the public sector, and the decision of whether to spend that much money is rooted in a variety of places, including good old-fashioned politics.

Nobody can deny that legislators probably get a lot more political mileage out of a ribbon-cutting ceremony for a new bridge than they do out of consolidating the state's data centers. Citizens understand the need for building bridges. Few people understand data center consolidation outside of a small circle of technologists, who often are not the best communicators.

But once a government entity decides to spend the money, it is management—good or bad—that is the determining factor between success and failure. It's rarely the case that the actual computers don't work when you plug them in. More often they just don't do what was wanted in the first place. Or they cost way too much. Or the people who are using them haven't been properly trained. Or the computer users have been trained, but on a different system. Or the new system takes five years to develop, by which time it's little more than a high-tech antique. Sometimes a new computer system works just great—but it can't communicate with any of the old systems.

A New Breed of Managers

Most of these technology problems can be prevented—if not solved—with smart, productive, efficient management. Yet, for years, agency and department officials, legislators, elected and appointed officials, and the whole range of men and women who keep government moving, have tried to avoid thinking hard about information technology. These government leaders hired smart people who could hypnotize them with talk of RAM and ROM, minicomputers and microcomputers, and megabytes and gigabytes.

Meanwhile, the computer experts often had little understanding of the way the new technology was going to be applied. They simply did not have the background to understand the business or service reasons behind the high-tech projects.

Fortunately, the days of managers who are ignorant about technology working with technologists who are ignorant about government are fading. Information technology has become potentially as critical an area as human resources or capital management for many city and state governments. And as such, information technology requires a new breed of managers—both those who have direct responsibility for IT operations and those for whom IT is an important element of their business plan.

Ironically, one of the unforeseen benefits of the Y2K bug scare in the late 1990s was that IT specialists traveled from agency to agency, remediating computer equipment. For many specialists, this was the first time they became exposed to what computers were actually being used for in the public sector and how it fit into the larger picture of government needs.

As Don Saelens, chief information officer of Minneapolis, said, "There is a tremendous awareness that IT isn't a back office operation. It's the front lines."

In Summary

- The speed of change in information technology has made speedy, careful management particularly critical.
- There's a real risk to going overboard with technology; if it doesn't have a clear business benefit, it's likely not a worthwhile investment.
- Examples of the benefits—both in terms of cash savings and improved service abound.
- Of course, cities and states that are cash short are going to have difficulties developing state-of-the-art IT systems; regardless of how effectively they manage.
- The political process, and the power struggles and chain of command that it requires, can be impediments to smooth function-

ing of IT offices—one major difference between the public and private sectors.

◆ A new breed of managers is necessary: technology experts who understand how government functions, and government managers who understand the benefits, costs, and risks of technology.

2

To Each His Own

"The future has to be invented every day," said Steve Kolodney, chief information officer of Washington state. "Best practices are short-lived and situational."

Kolodney is a smart fellow, and he's speaking from experience. The simple, though disappointing truth is that the only overriding guideline for success in implementing information technology is that there is no single overriding guideline that guarantees success in the field.

One size fits all may be a lovely concept when it comes to baseball caps, but it's a prescription for disaster in IT.

What's more, a great IT management idea in 2000 may be a has-been concept in 2001, and an antiquated one in 2002. There's a rule of thumb that technology enters a whole new generation every eighteen months. Like most rules of thumb, this one doesn't deserve intense scrutiny. But anyone who has purchased a home computer in the past few years knows the frustration that comes with buying something in September, only to find that there's something even better available in January; at a lower price.

This is not an easy concept for cities and states to get their bureaucratic arms around. When a city buys a fleet of new cruisers for its police department, there's every reason to believe that the cars will not be much cheaper in the following year. And they're certainly not going to become twice as fast by burning half the gasoline. But that's exactly the case with computing power.

So, governments need to be unusually (perhaps impossibly) nimble in purchasing technology.

Varying Goals

Moreover, although learning from the experiences of other entities is always a good idea—why reinvent the floppy disk?—the goals that governments are trying to achieve vary from city to city and state to state.

Consider kiosks for example. Dozens of cities and states have been bragging proudly about all the amazing stuff their residents can do at kiosks. Oregon officials proudly point out that the state's Employment Department has placed more than 100 touch-screen kiosks around the state that provide job listings.

Maryland's statewide master plan for IT—a visionary statement that the state is using to guide its efforts for the next half-decade or so—clearly specifies that the state wants to have more kiosks in place for a variety of activities.

So, then, kiosks are a good idea, right? Sure they are. At least for Oregon and Maryland (and hundreds of other places).

But consider the state of Washington. It's been a pioneer in the use of Web-based technology. Several years ago Washington had already advanced to the point where Maryland wants to be in the next few years. It had plenty of kiosks to provide information to people in remote areas of the state. (Washington's pioneering status is illustrated by its Internet addresses. If you send e-mail to a state government employee in Washington, for example someone named John Smith, his address will be something like *jsmith@dis.wa.gov*. It's those last three letters that are the giveaway. "Gov" was used by all governments early on in the development of the Internet. Then, it became the exclusive province of the federal government; and only the states and cities that were in Internet development early on were grandfathered in.)

But Washington didn't hesitate to shut down IT services that weren't in sufficient demand ("like a business," said Kolodney). When enough citizens had access to the Internet, the state decided to shut down the kiosks, preferring to reach taxpayers in their living rooms.

Okay, then kiosks are good—and replacing kiosks with personal computers is even better—right? Wrong again, for some states. In

South Dakota, where the population is spread out over a lot of land, the state's CIO, Otto Doll, has something different to say about kiosks. "Having people go to the town hall, from 100 miles away, whether it's to register to vote or register their car or whatever; the last thing they want to do is walk up to a machine. We're stuck with the fact that when they do come in they want to talk to a human. And they can't do it from home because they don't have a computer. Only about 15 percent of our population is Web enabled."

North Carolinians feel the same way. Their state did a survey in 1998, involving twelve focus groups. Citizens said they really want to use services offered over the Internet. But they indicated that they are very concerned about being able to really talk to a human being. "They don't want kiosks," said one official there. "They want to be able to talk to a clerk."

It isn't difficult to see that geographically spread out states like South Dakota or Wyoming have different needs than tiny ones like Rhode Island or Connecticut. Large population centers such as New York, Chicago, or Los Angeles don't share the same needs as mid-sized cities such as New Haven, Connecticut, or Evanston, Illinois. And New Haven and Evanston have different needs from even smaller cities and towns, including those that are too small to appear on most maps.

The Need for Stakeholder Input

But while all that may seem to be self-evident, there's a certain "keeping up with the Joneses" aspect to any kind of high technology planning. And with all due respect to the men and women who are more technologist than manager, there can be an overpowering desire to buy the latest, spiffiest, sharpest new piece of technology around—to live on what's been described as the bleeding edge. So, if kiosks are hot, then kiosks get bought.

The key to making sure that Minneapolis isn't just trying to keep up with St. Paul, and North Dakota isn't copying South Dakota is for IT managers at all levels to keep close tabs on all the stakeholders involved; this includes agencies, legislatures, end-users (including, essentially, everyone who has contact with a computer), citizens, and groups that represent them.

Sadly, such communications with stakeholders is not sufficiently common. And if there's any single lesson to be learned in this chapter, it's that communication is crucial. One large city, for example, recently put in a complex system that was intended to allow judges who rule on parking violations to quickly access a great deal of information that would help them to adjudicate cases quickly and fairly. Unfortunately, the judges themselves seem to have been left out of the decision as to precisely how this software was to function. As a result, the end product resulted in more grumbling than pleasure among their corps.

Perhaps the most extreme example of technology being created with insufficient advance discussion can be found in the Web sites established by many cities and states. Far more on this point will be found in Chapter 12. But one clear truth is that these sites have often been established with little attention for the real desires of their users.

South Carolina was one exception here: it did a survey of its populace before putting together the statewide Web site, and to the surprise of many discovered that the information about state jobs was the top priority. Designers then put extensive effort into the Web site's job page, ensuring that potential applicants could search by salary level, agency, type, and geographic area and have hyperlinks to such related topics as the the state's temporary employment service.

Of course, once information is gathered from stakeholders, there's rarely going to be a consensus of opinion. And that's where the normal managerial processes for decision making come into action. But the temptation to ignore facts because they might confuse the issue should be avoided. The more information available, the greater the likelihood that a state's IT will turn out to be as useful as money permits.

In Summary

◆ It's reasonable to anticipate that any idea, however sensible this year, will be out of date a couple of years from now.

- There is no "one-size-fits-all" solution to IT needs.
- Needs depend on population, geographic diversity, and other variables.
- It's not wise to buy technology simply because neighboring states or cities are doing so.
- The best way to tailor technology for individual needs is through thorough stakeholder input.

3

Land Mines in Project Management

Technology promises to transform the way governments do business, create new paths for citizen access, eliminate repetitive clerical jobs, and enhance intergovernmental cooperation. And it can do all that.

Technology can also make grown men and women scream in anguish. The apparent inevitability of some kind of snafu in any significant IT project led one state IT manager to suggest, tongue-in-cheek, that the following is the typical life-cycle of a project:

1. Wild enthusiasm
2. Utter confusion
3. Deep disappointment
4. Search for the guilty
5. Punishment of the loyal
6. Promotion of the uninvolved

On Time and on Budget?

Practically every day a scan of the nation's headlines reveals some state, city, or county that is struggling with a disaster in the making. In 1999 major computer crises were under the spotlight in Los Angeles, where an integrated human resources system was plagued with technical and management problems, costing the city some $20 million with little to show for its investment. In Nebraska, a project to help determine welfare eligibility in the Health and Human Services Department cost $70 million—nearly five times as much as was originally planned. After spending all that money, the project still wasn't working right.

And the stories keep coming. A survey of headlines in the last two weeks of March 2000 revealed:

♦ How county officials in Ravalli County, Montana, had to take at least $100,000 from reserve funds to pay to replace the courthouse computer network that they recently discovered had unsafe wiring and was poorly designed.

♦ How campaign-reporting software, which cost the state of Missouri about $500,000 in installation costs and another $5,000 a month, still did not work, although the contract was signed three years before and the law required Internet reporting as of January 1998.

♦ How hundreds of thousands of motorists across Florida might not receive auto license tag renewal notices because the wrong addresses were loaded into a new computer at the state Department of Highway Safety and Motor Vehicles. According to the *St. Petersburg Times,* the problem started when a new state computer was brought on-line and merged several huge databases.

In the mid-1990s, a study by a market research and consulting firm, the Standish Group International, concluded that of IT projects that cost more than $10 million—in both public and private sectors—virtually none were completed "on time, on budget, and with all of the features and functions originally specified."

Of course, that study was several years ago when the technology was new to a lot of people. Today, IT project managers are more experienced and are having a little more success. What's more, the expectation that any long-range project—whether technologically oriented or not—is completed "on time, on budget, and with all the features and functions originally specified"—is a high standard in any field. If you ever have had a house built, you know it is a lot less complicated than a major computer installation, and unless you're

Bill Gates, a lot cheaper. But odds are that at some point in the process, the plans were changed, you wound up having to spend more, and the kitchen cabinets took six weeks longer to install than you'd been told. Even the book you're holding in your hands at this very moment took months more than originally anticipated, and there were a couple of chapters jettisoned along the way because they proved to be impractical. (It did come in on budget, however—but that's only because publishers simply haven't heard of renegotiating contracts.)

There's an important distinction between the headaches described above—the kind that get a lot of attention—and the ordinary, run-of-the-mill problems that also populated the Standish Group's findings. Neither is desirable, but while a multimillion-dollar cost overrun is fodder for legislative carping, people seem to take in stride the more ubiquitous kind of technology irritants like slogging software, network downtime, and improperly input data.

While any government involved in technology can expect its share of a variety of problems, there's a great deal that can be done to help avoid them. In the study of eighty-five government entities in the GPP, a great many problems in management were mentioned. However, when it came to problems with specific projects, the issue mentioned most frequently was inadequate project management.

Underestimating Scope at the Outset

Ironically, one of the most significant shortcomings in project management often begins before managers are assigned to the project. In GPP interviews, managers repeatedly complained that they had been handed a project to implement that hadn't been given sufficient thought at the outset. Agencies anxious for a new piece of technology (and this even includes entity-wide systems) are prone to be overly optimistic about the simplicity of projects. These agencies often don't consider potential—and inevitable—bugs in implementation.

The resultant problems are twofold: chronic underestimating of the cost of a project and the amount of time it will take to implement a new system.

In Baltimore, managers complain that a great frustration has been "the amount of time required to develop, implement, integrate, and successfully debut new hardware and software systems." Discussing the new Enterprise Resource Planning System, Elliot Schlanger, CIO, noted that it was running about six months behind schedule. Explained Schlanger, "Like many ERP projects in this world that happened to precede it, when we began, both the contractor and the city underestimated the scope of what, in fact, a project like this would entail."

Underestimating a project's scope was also cited as a problem by Richard McKinney, the new IT director in Nashville, for the very long time it took to implement the new financial management system there. "It looks to me like at first they underestimated the size of what it would require to implement a system-wide system," McKinney said.

This reason was also given to *Governing* reporter Ellen Perlman as one explanation for the problems that plagued California's Youth and Adult Correctional Agency's plans for a $40 million integrated electronic inmate records system. The system was ultimately scrapped and the state filed suit against the prime contractor citing delays, higher projected costs, and fewer features than originally promised. The vendor TRW claimed the corrections agency "made a gross underestimation of the project's size and complexity" and that TRW had relied upon those "misrepresentations" in arriving at its fixed-price bid.

It's not difficult to understand why underestimating costs and implementation time happens so frequently in IT projects. Human nature plays a big role; when an agency head wants something badly enough, it's easy to turn a deaf ear to those who are advising caution and listen instead to the zealots. Smart managers avoid this temptation. What's more, many of the problems that raise costs and extend time spans are genuinely unpredictable in the world of IT. Unlike many capital projects (putting up a new office building, for example), IT efforts are often unlike any that have ever been done before. Even off-the-shelf software must be integrated with systems unique to a particular city or a state. With IT, there's a new variation on Murphy's Law. Let's call it Custer's Law, in honor of that talented Civil

War general who grossly underestimated the potential of the Native Americans at Little Big Horn: "If anything can go wrong," Custer's Law indicates, "it won't be something you anticipated."

Scope Creep

Sometimes, it's not that managers underestimated the problems with a project at the outset; it's that the project turned into a microchip-laden snowball rolling downhill; growing as it advanced. Experienced IT professionals call this phenomenon "scope creep." Tennessee's CIO, Bradley Dugger, explained, "It's when someone says they want to do a significant application—payroll, for example. Someone may come in and say we want to do a payroll system, where we pay all our active employees, but by the time you're finished, it's also paying retirees and locals. You keep adding stuff to it; you're building a building, but you keep adding floors. The problem is getting people to define this is the problem I'm trying to solve and not come back later and say I forgot to tell you this."

IT professionals indicate that the best way to prevent scope creep is to clearly define a project before a dollar is spent. At heart, this involves ensuring that clear business objectives are identified. This involves inviting all the potential stakeholders in for discussion, to make quite certain that a constituency isn't going to be ignored in initial plans, only to have its voice heard loud and clear later on. But at heart, scope creep can only be prevented with project managers who demonstrate resolute, strong leadership, and—who are, in turn, backed up by their superiors.

A Shortage of Project Managers

The three crucial elements for a successful IT project that the Standish Group identified were (1) clear business objectives, (2) executive support, and (3) an experienced project manager

We've touched on the first two above; and there will be more information about them in subsequent chapters. The third, however, is one of the most difficult for public sector entities to deal with. Experienced project managers are in extremely short supply.

This basic truth—that it's difficult to hire and even more difficult to retain good people for these jobs—has several unpleasant side effects.

1. Horses are always being changed midstream. People often leave projects before they're finished.
2. Time-intensive activities such as planning get short-changed.
3. Unqualified employees are given jobs they don't have the experience to handle.

Yet another side effect of having an insufficient number of trained project managers is that some managers are willing to fob off the job on the companies hired, instead of retaining the responsibility internally. Baltimore's CIO, Elliot Schlanger described this type of situation: "I would say this, at risk of getting into a little bit of trouble; the city needs to go through a learning process of how to manage its independent contractors, or contractors in general. [You often hear the excuse] that the contractor was late in delivering; and it's almost as though there is a divorce of responsibility where the city doesn't perceive they have any ownership. But even though we may use contractors, the city has the responsibility in terms of ownership and accountability."

Training Project Managers

Why is it so difficult to find good project managers? One northeastern CIO put part of the problem succinctly. "[States are not] competitive when it comes to attracting people with those skills" he said. "The benefits aren't the same as you would find in the IT industry." While it's true that at least a quarter of cities and states in the GPP are currently adjusting pay levels for IT workers generally—including project managers—the fact is that using cash to compete with the private sector for the best and brightest is often a losing game.

Fortunately, research has shown that pay is not the only reason people choose to work for the public sector. Many other factors attract people to these jobs, not the least of which is an altruistic sense that they are doing something good for their fellow citizen.

With that in mind, the key is to help the people you're able to hire to do their jobs as well as possible. And that leads, inevitably to efforts to better train project managers. That's just the direction many states and cities are heading in. Kansas, for example, has been implementing project management standards and training. State officials have a customized text that's used to train project managers. And the training leads to professional certification.

Michigan's CIO George Boersma is taking a similar approach. "One of the things that we created was the office of project managers. If you want to be a project manager in IT, you're going to have to have certain training before you can do that."

Why Bad Things Happen to Project Managers

Sometimes, problems crop up because the project managers weren't adequately trained or skilled. But there are a whole host of other factors that can conspire to keep the IT troops marching forward, ever forward, until ultimately they fall off the edge of a cliff. Here are a few common occurrences that can trip up project managers:

◆ As Ellen Perlman pointed out in her September 1998 *Governing* article, entitled "Technotrouble," sometimes agencies "try to camouflage the difficulties involved in a risky, complicated project so as not to scare off a desirable contractor."

◆ There can be gamesmanship between various contractors involved in putting together a system. None of them wants to confront a problem because that might mean they were partially responsible. As a result, contractors hide their knowledge until it's too late.

◆ Weak communication between the government and the contractor.

◆ Fear. This is probably the single most troublesome issue in government work. It's not hard to see the enormous pressure on project managers to keep quiet when things seem headed in the wrong direction. When a government spends money, the pressure to move projects forward is immense. Political careers can be hurt by costly foul-ups. And politicians are eager to see projects completed during their tenure (even if they blow up on the next guy's watch).

How to Stop Bad Things from Happening to Project Managers

Beyond proper training of project managers, there are some other reasonable efforts under way to help them do their jobs well. In a number of states and cities, for example, managers are required to report project status to the legislature and administration at regular intervals. "What we're really looking for is accountability," Nebraska's Tom Conroy said. "We've taken a large project and shown how it can be managed in a way that people don't have to get into details, but report where the bumps in the road are."

California is taking this a step further by prequalifying consulting firms to provide a thumbs up or down at various stages of technology projects. All major projects now undergo independent verification and validation by outside consultants.

Another reform put in place by California is that each project has "an executive sponsor" within the agency who can keep attention focused on what's going on. "We want to make sure we don't fall back to large, large projects with an indeterminate scope and no sponsor," California's CIO John Thomas Flynn told *Governing*.

It's also beneficial for cities and states to encourage project managers to point out potential problems as early on as possible. For one thing, there's no disgrace in killing a project outright, particularly if that can be done before spending the entire budget allocated for it. "Neither the CIO nor administration has a second thought about walking away from a project that doesn't work," said Courtney Harrington, deputy director, Department of Information Technology in Honolulu.

Better yet, projects can sometimes be salvaged before they reach stage three of the tongue-in-cheek life-cycle that begins this chapter: "Deep disappointment."

Phoenix, for example, delayed its new budget system for about a year—a decision that managers say was ultimately extremely beneficial for the city. In this case, the project manager was experienced.

He came from the business arena, had worked on other implementations, and understood the implications of putting in the system prematurely.

Even though it worked functionally, the software wasn't powerful enough for the size of the operation. "We just didn't find out till we loaded the system and tried to operate it," one manager there said. "The system performed so slowly that the feeling was that there would be dissatisfaction." So, resources were dedicated to upgrading the software so that it would perform as well as expected. "It's just not a good idea to turn on a system that doesn't meet someone's needs," said one IT source in Phoenix.

In Summary

◆ Many large problems in information technology have been the result of inadequate project management.
◆ One major problem is underestimating the time required for a project and its cost at the outset. Managers anxious to get a project rolling may well be complicit in purposefully ignoring potential problems.
◆ In other instances, the scope of a project continues to grow as time goes on; often a symptom of inadequate advance planning or too little consultation with stakeholders in the project's design.
◆ Experienced project managers are key to success; unfortunately they are in short supply.
◆ Because government entities cannot easily compete with the private sector in paying project managers, it's wise for the public sector to look to internal training.
◆ Even well-trained project managers can run into difficulties for a variety of reasons; many of them linked to fear of being blamed for the problems they point out.
◆ As a result, it's in the best interest of cities and states to make it easier for project managers to uncover—and report—emerging problems, before they become full-fledged disasters.

4

Lurching Toward the Center

One great riddle for cities, states, and counties is how to set up a structure for technology planning, procurement, and oversight that provides sufficient central control and yet doesn't constrain innovation or ignore differences among agencies. Stacks of scholarly works about government management and structure give guidance—though most pertain to subjects other than technology.

But one source, rarely found in government libraries, seems to shed bright light on this area. In the following excerpt from that source a few words have been changed, but the thrust of the argument is unaltered: "Strictness or permissiveness is not the real issue. Central IT offices that aren't afraid to be firm when it is necessary can get good results with either moderate strictness or moderate permissiveness. On the other hand, a strictness that comes from harsh feelings or a permissiveness that is timid or vacillating can each lead to poor results. The real issue is what spirit the government puts into managing its IT, and what attitude is engendered in the agencies as a result."

The source? The fortieth edition of Dr. Spock's *Baby and Child Care.* The only alterations from the actual quote in the book were to substitute "Central IT offices" and "government" for the "parents" and "agencies" for children.

Of course, Dr. Spock's words somewhat oversimplify the task (though much of his advice about children pertains to computers, such as "forget about the qualities that they don't have"). Still, his approach applies just as sensibly to technology in the public sector as it does to rearing well-adjusted children. According to Carl Meyers, assistant IT director of Phoenix: "There isn't one right answer. It's a function of what works best for the organization and what its vision is."

When the Mainframes Ruled

The history of governmental organization of technology has been one of wild swings during the last couple of decades between autocratic centralized management structures and decentralized (and often fragmented) efforts. There's still a lot of tension over this question, though the majority of states and cities surveyed by the GPP indicated that they were groping toward some kind of a hybrid structure.

As technology blossomed in the 1970s, power was often lodged in mainframe shops where the technocrats ruled. This was, of course, a time when the idea that every secretary would have a desktop computer seemed like something out of *The Jetsons,* the futuristic cartoon of the 1960s. Nontechnologically oriented managers hadn't yet seen the overwhelming importance that information technology would soon have in their organizations. IT basically meant the use of mainframe computers, which were the exclusive province of people who knew how to run them.

As a result—and patient readers will please forgive another nongovernmental reference—they lived in a world much like that described by H. G. Wells in *The Time Machine.* In that wonderful book, Wells describes a future in which two species of human have emerged. Those conversant with technology live underground, speak their own language, and keep all the machinery for the planet running.

Meanwhile, the rest of humankind live in happy indifference to the way any of the mechanisms worked, oblivious to the sacrifices they were making for their indifference. (Of course, unlike H. G. Wells's grim version of the future, there's no evidence that the technologists of the 1970s actually turned cannibalistic.)

The problem, of course, with turning technology over to folks who understand the machines, but not necessarily the governments they're intended to serve, is that it is unlikely that the technocrats can serve their governments well.

Decentralization—and Its Problems

Richard McKinney, director of technology in the city of Nashville, describes the evolution in his city: "When it was a mainframe shop, the guy who ran it was autocratic, and he charged the agencies large amounts to run data. He told the customers what they were supposed to want."

As obviously flawed as this approach was, it was mirrored in a great many other entities at the same time. And it was doomed by the arrival of new, cheaper advances in computerization that allowed individual agencies to run their own systems, and ultimately tie desktops into more powerful, centrally located computers in client-server systems. Why follow the dictates of some fellow who doesn't understand your agency, when you can go out and buy your very own equipment?

Vendors were only too happy to take advantage of this built-up frustration. McKinney, who is hard at work trying to fix a variety of IT problems in the Tennessee capital recounted: "Once the 80s rolled around, vendors would come in and say, 'I've got a box right here that will get you everything you need.' So, agencies said, 'We can do better than we've been doing.' They figured out the cost, and said, 'We can pay for that box.'"

It's no surprise that an overwhelming number of cities and states chose to move toward decentralization during the last two decades. And this, in and of itself, was not a bad thing. However, those cities and states that went too far in this direction—losing crucial vestiges of central authority—gave up at least as much as they gained. In fact, the four cities that received the lowest grades in the GPP city survey—taking into account all the areas studied—Atlanta, Columbus, Dallas, and Nashville—all had a history of deep decentralization, though they all were in various stages of change. By the same token, the cities that fared the best—Minneapolis, Phoenix,

Honolulu, and Philadelphia—all have powerful planning and control emanating from centralized authorities while encouraging creativity at the agency level.

The problems with inadequate central controls are easy to uncover and just begin with a tendency to wind up with a patchwork approach to IT. "You tend to have a redundancy of systems because everybody thinks they're unique," said one IT manager in Houston. "And that's a problem because you lose the true repository of all the information and the ability to go out there and collect it, because there are so many places to go get it."

Then there's the potential disparity between agencies that are better funded and those with less cash in the coffers. Gary Langhoff, former budget director of Milwaukee, explained, "It created a rift between the haves and have nots. You had departments with control of more resources that could buy more. And you had departments that couldn't and they were left trailing in the dust. It didn't make sense to let money make those decisions." A reorganization of city departments in Milwaukee over the past year has centralized much IT funding, which has helped eliminate this problem.

In any case, the total cost in tax dollars rises dramatically the more decentralized the process is. In Columbus, for example, "Departments have been autonomous," one former city official reported. "They built their own systems. Sometimes they communicate with each other and other times they don't. The e-mail and word processing and office products alone, cost more than they had to, just because they weren't coordinated."

Similarly, in the state of Hawaii, according to the State of Hawaii Information Technology Overview, "departments and agencies have been allowed to develop their own capabilities for implementing and managing their IT assets." As a result, everyone reinvents the wheel and each department tries to establish its own technical experts and pool of knowledge. This increases IT costs overall, according to Barbara Tom, former planning and project management officer in the Information and Communication Services Division.

Another additional cost can come when agencies don't have the expertise to make the IT decisions but don't want to rely on the central office for advice. As a result they often turn to consultants, who are only too happy to charge hundreds of dollars an hour to replicate expertise that already exists in-house.

In Search of a Middle Ground

Fortunately, a number of cities and states have recognized the problems with extreme decentralization of IT management. The hope, of course, is that their historic memory is deep and broad enough that they will find a middle ground.

Dwight Dively, finance director in Seattle, summed up the effort nicely: "The city has done pendulum swings from the days when there was a committee that needed to approve every PC that was bought; to basically where departments had free reign; and now to movement back toward the middle."

Milwaukee is another city that has had a decentralized structure and is moving to a more centralized one. Langhoff explained, "Everybody wants to retain the best parts that distributed computing has given us—because it has fostered a lot of innovation and creativity in departments. What we don't want to do is go back to some kind of IT dark ages, which is what existed in the early 90s, where you have this monolithic structure saying, 'No you can't do that. Yes you can do that.' We need to allow departments to do what they need to do. And to have this organization there in the midst of this making sure the process fit together."

Michigan's CIO, George Boersma echoed this belief: "You have to go and balance centralization, with empowering the local people. We don't want to sit here and put the iron hand down and say everybody's going to do this at a certain time. We're looking at three different categories: something that is unique to an agency and only that agency can use. Something that falls in a core process that other agencies can use; something that falls into the infrastructure of the state as a whole." That kind of multitiered approach seems to be a key toward success in this area.

For example, Phoenix in the late 1980s began planning for its move away from a decentralized environment—"islands of automation," one official there called them—in which departments employed whatever technology served their departments needs. At that time, Phoenix had disparate computer applications and e-mail systems that limited citywide data sharing and communications. To share information, paper copies had to be duplicated and distributed or files copied onto diskettes and delivered.

The city then set about shifting to a coordinated-decentralized approach or "federated republic" management structure. The underlying logic: if more than one department needed access to an IT function, an enterprise-wide solution was warranted. Otherwise, with oversight from the central office, the agency was given significantly more latitude in making its choice.

The city's Information Technology Department is responsible for establishing citywide technology standards, policies, and guidelines as well as establishing Phoenix's information technology architecture framework. But in order to keep the agencies firmly in that loop, the city has employed a system of information technology contacts in every department. These contacts evaluate new or revised policies and standards; disseminate information to departments and share information and experiences with other departments. Every department has a local area network administrator as well. Today, with the "coordinated decentralized" approach, departmental barriers and control issues have all but faded away.

Other cities and states have followed in similar paths. In Austin, Texas, the Information Services office is responsible for citywide direction; policies and procedures for technology that crosses departmental needs, such as infrastructure, desktop hardware, and software standards; voice systems; and citywide applications such as e-mail. Departments manage technology that is department-specific, such as the reservation system used at the parks and recreation department. "The balance we need to strike is (between) control and flexibility," said John Stephens, former acting chief information officer in Austin.

Sufficient Central Authority

It's tempting to end this chapter right here, by advocating a balance between decentralized authority and central control. But in the real world, this isn't always so simple.

One problem is that in many localities, the central office simply doesn't have the authority to do its job properly. In Mississippi, one official explained, "We don't tell the agencies what they have to do. That's not within our mission."

In Los Angeles, Jim House, chief administrative analyst added: "You've got to be cognizant of the political realities and commitments. We aren't a real vertical organization where the reporting structure is clearly defined. It's much more diffuse, you have to use the combination of carrot and stick. You don't have the choice of dictating what will be done."

Arkansas has moved clearly in the path of maintaining more central control over the agencies' IT decisions. Yet, according to Earl Norton, who works in the auditor's office there, "There are still factions out there who aren't satisfied—but I tend to think those particular people are anarchists at heart, and they want their own bank accounts. They want no centralized anything, and they want no accountability for it."

A couple of years ago, while Nevada was approving an integrated financial system for the state as a whole, its Department of Transportation made a budget request for its own financial management system. The state's director of the Department of Information Technology recalled, "I was called to comment and asked directly whether we should be doing this. And I said, 'Absolutely not. This is exactly the kind of redundancy we're trying to avoid.' You can appreciate how unpopular I was. It created some difficulties; hurt some relationships."

What emerges clearly is that the road back from decentralization is rarely one that can be moved on quickly. Agency heads need to see that it will benefit them. They need to be confident that they're not going to have policies or equipment that will be forced upon them.

Richard Wilken, director of information technology and communications in San Diego explained, "We're in a transition from a decentralized governance process to one that is more centralized, but we have to do it in a logical order so we have support for it."

Perhaps the most significant key in accomplishing such a successful transition is accepting the notion that a successful structure requires both strong leadership—preferably in the form of a chief information officer—and an openness to input from all the parties who will be affected by the CIO's actions. Much detail about how this process should work can be found in the next chapter.

Of course, experimentation with leadership and central control continues with various cities and states making new efforts on a regular basis—sometimes with success, other times failing. This business of managing IT is still new enough that new models are still of real interest and value.

In Summary

◆ The balance between central controls and decentralized authority in the agency is difficult to manage.

◆ In the 1970s, power was lodged in often autocratic mainframe shops that controlled computing power in many cities and states. However, when desktops and client/server systems became available, many entities decentralized. Vendors were happy to encourage this process.

◆ Decentralization, in and of itself, is not a bad thing. It can help encourage innovation and creativity. But, taken too far it can lead to redundant systems; disparity between richer and poorer agencies; a lack of communication between agencies; increased costs of maintenance and training; increased procurement costs and the need for consultants who may duplicate resources already in house.

◆ Realizing the problems of decentralization, many cities and states are now groping for a middle ground that balances the empowerment and innovation of decentralization with the efficiencies of centralization.

◆ Phoenix's "federated republic" approach is a good model of how this kind of middle ground can be reached.

◆ In order for a balance to be reached, the central office must be given sufficient authority to make decisions and to enforce them. It also needs to get buy-in from agencies to do this.

5
Who's in Charge?

For years, no large city or state would consider functioning without a chief financial officer and someone to head up the personnel department. Yet, until very recently, many local governments pushed relentlessly forward purchasing and implementing technology without an equivalent position. Luckily, this situation is changing. A number of cities and states have appointed their first chief information officers (CIOs) in just the past few years. Although not every government entity calls this new position a CIO, the concept is the same: one person who oversees policy-making, standardization, and oversight for the organization.

Among those that have recently taken this step are the states of Alabama, Kentucky, Nebraska, and New Jersey and the cities of Dallas, Milwaukee, and San Diego. According to Richard Wilken, information technology and communications director in San Diego, "The impact of technology and what it can offer us is much more significant now than it was ten years ago, and it's time to elevate the management."

Some entities continue to argue that they do not need a formal CIO position, but the Government Performance Project found a powerful correlation between the presence of that job and good management of IT otherwise. Among the management efforts that most clearly benefited from the existence of a CIO were strategic planning; efforts toward building a coherent standardized architecture; and the capacity to evaluate the extent to which benefits of an information technology system justified investment.

A few years ago, Baltimore's mayor determined that there were many shortcomings in his city's information technology management. He set up an information technology board, which was made up of his chief of staff and four key agency heads in the city, and charged them with coordinating technology needs. Among the board's first steps was to appoint a CIO. Elliot Schlanger, who was given that post, noted that before he came, there was a central MIS operation, but that without a leadership position with power and authority in the government at large, it was not managed well.

What Should a CIO Do?

The trick here is to ensure that the CIO should be a genuinely strategic, oversight position for the entity as a whole. This does not mean that the CIO should be personally responsible for controlling the individual agencies. In fact as discussed in Chapter 4, the more independence agencies can be given, the better off they probably are. The crucial elements of a successful CIO's post, instead, are to:

◆ Ensure that agencies are held accountable to delivering the promised benefits of any IT expenditures.
◆ Coordinate the efforts of the various agencies in some kind of statewide strategic plan for IT.
◆ Make certain that agencies work together toward common goals in a way that isn't duplicative or counterproductive.
◆ Act as a conduit between the chief executive officer (and, with luck the legislative branch as well) and the agencies, when it comes to IT decision making.
◆ Help to develop standards or an architecture for the state that precludes stovepipe systems that do not work well together.

Of course, many CIOs have come up through the technological ranks, and that will continue to be the case. And a basic understanding of technology—what it can and cannot do and where the potential trouble spots lie—is important. But even more important are the managerial/political skills required to manage a large cadre of workers and to relate effectively with governors, mayors, legislators, citizens, and all the other stakeholders who play a role in this field.

The heart of this notion was well articulated by *Governing*'s publisher and editor, Peter Harkness in the June 1999 issue of that magazine: "Technology management has moved from the computer room to the board room."

One trap some localities fall into is assuming that their new CIO can do two jobs at once. "I've seen a lot of cities who have taken their IT director and just renamed it a CIO," said Virginia Beach CIO David Sullivan. "The IT director already had sixty hours a week of work to do. I realized if that were the case here, I couldn't get at the strategic issues. It would do no good to call me the CIO and expect me to deal with those issues and others. So, we brought in a new IT director to handle the department. It's worked out very well."

Another large city just hired its second CIO. The person who took the job—who for obvious reasons won't be named here—was startled to discover that in his first week, he was getting all manner of phone calls related to problems with specific pieces of equipment in city agencies. One of his first steps in the new job will be going to the city and asking for money to simulate the kind of arrangement Sullivan has.

Where Do CIOs Belong in the Leadership Chart?

This leads directly to one of the most significant questions regarding CIOs. Who should they report to? Generally, the answer is that the CIO should be a cabinet-level position, reporting to the mayor or city manager, governor, or county commissioners. One CIO pointed out the incongruity in placing his job lower down on the management food chain: "Information Technology has become such an integral part of business. But it isn't viewed that way because I have another level to go through."

Among cities and states in which the CIO reports directly to the top are: Connecticut, Delaware, Iowa, Kentucky, Minnesota, Missouri, Honolulu, Long Beach, Los Angeles, Nashville, Richmond, San Diego, and San Jose.

In some others the CIO may not report directly to the top, but is a cabinet position, which is sensible enough. In Kentucky's organizational charts, in fact, the CIO position actually falls above cabinet level.

But the one rule for government management that is inviolate is that any general rule has a number of exceptions. Cities and states, with widely varying needs and structures have to take those factors into account. In New York City, for instance, the CIO reports to a deputy mayor. When New York's CIO was asked if he felt slighted by being a step away from the pinnacle of power in the nation's largest city he chortled, "I couldn't think of anything that would make me less efficient than that. The mayor has a thousand things to do. The deputy mayor has the time. Every week I have a meeting with him. And every other week, I have an extra meeting. There's no way our mayor could do that."

In other places, there's concern that reporting to the governor could politicize the position. Thomas Towle, director of the Division of Information Technology Management in New Hampshire explained the political drawbacks of high placement: "One of the difficulties when the CIO reports to the governor's office is it becomes a political position. We have a governor's election every two years. [Being placed in the department of administrative services] brings it back to continuity and consistency."

In one southern state, the IT department reports to the Department of Commerce. At first blush this seems foolish (and, in fact, there may be a better place for it). But the logic behind the decision makes sense. The director of that department is considered a very good manager and wasn't overloaded, as were other directors in the government. As for the governor, one insider reported, "He's interested in welfare reform or increasing teacher pay. A lot of things he's interested in aren't at the level of IT. If you have a governor who is interested in IT, and that's important, then it may work well, if it doesn't, you may get lost quick in the shuffle."

It would certainly appear that a reasonably powerful CIO is important. None of the states with strong CIOs have plans to weaken the position. Yet a number of states with somewhat weak CIOs (who report to someone other than the governor, have little control over budgeting decisions, or are seriously understaffed) are talking about elevating the position.

But although there can be rational logic to the CIO not reporting directly to the top, the overwhelming evidence—if only anecdotally—from the GPP is that the higher the placement of the job, the better the results. In fact, while some entities made arguments, as illustrated above, that their top technology officer was able to do his or her job well without reporting to the mayor or governor, not one individual complained that his or her job should be shoved lower down the management chart.

One warning: while the CIO's position is crucial, there's a real danger in equating a powerful, smart chief information officer with a technologically well-run state or city. One private sector vendor recently argued vociferously that focusing too much on the CIO is "missing the boat." He continued, "I sell millions of dollars worth of equipment to governments, and I couldn't care less about the CIOs. They may be setting policy, but it's down at the agency level that the real important stuff is happening."

Some Model CIO Positions

Allowing for the idea that differences in cities and states make flexibility a crucial commodity, it's worth a quick look at the specifics of the CIO position in four of the states that received the highest overall grades for information technology in the 1999 edition of the Government Performance Project:

◆ **Utah.** The CIO provides centralized oversight coordinating information technology across the agencies. The position is housed in the governor's office, is a cabinet-level position that reports directly to the governor, and has statutory responsibility for approval of IT budgets, departmental IT plans, and coordination of IT policies and standards across the executive branch.
◆ **Washington.** The CIO is also a cabinet-level position and has the authority to pull the plug on a failing technology project. He or she also has direct control over the agencies' IT budgets. What's more, if the state is providing services that aren't in

demand, it's within his or her authority to shut them down, like an antiquated business.

◆ **Virginia.** The powerful CIO's authority goes beyond just internal operations. It combines operational authority for developing, acquiring, and operating a state-of-the-art operation in the state with working with the private sector to create an environment that attracts technology-related businesses to the state.

◆ **Missouri.** Again, the CIO reports to the governor, and all IT budget requests go to the CIO's office before they get to the governor's office. Missouri's current CIO described his place in the hierarchy, "We own purchasing and the IT budget. I have purposefully avoided becoming the project director for all projects, but if one is in trouble, I take action on it. I try to get along with the departments and their IT directors. But, at worst, I can go to the governor and say this has to be killed."

Bringing in the Stakeholders

In fact, as stated in the previous chapter, wherever the CIO reports in the organizational chart—or even if there is no CIO altogether—one of the major tasks that the central IT office must perform well is to ensure that the agencies and other stakeholders feel involved in the process. The power of a bureaucracy to stand in the way of even the most sensible initiative can't be overstated. But if you've got the agencies and departments in synch, all kinds of land mines can be avoided. This has often been successfully accomplished through some kind of advisory council, as is found in the states of Maryland and North Carolina, the cities of Kansas City, Long Beach, and Washington, D.C., and a growing number of other localities. The composition of these boards varies, but they often include representatives from agencies and the legislature.

Tony Herbert, administrator of the Information Services Division in Montana, explained, "It might be a lot easier with a benevolent dictator type-model. But we've painfully learned that involving your users pays extraordinary dividends. You don't have to go back on decisions and make them right [after you've run into resistance]. We used a benevolent dictator model prior to 1990. And in

1990, our Information Technology Advisory Council emerged as a more willing and more powerful entity."

Not that such committees don't have their downside: "It slows the process a good deal," said Herbert. "There are issues you have to stop and walk through with these people. It's frustrating for me and my people. We are often on the right track, but it might take a month or two or more to work through issues with them, to make sure we have that full-fledged support. But as much frustration as that presents for a guy like me and my key managers, I think we're ending up with much better results."

Baltimore also employs its so-called information technology board as a "voice of consensus for the city," said its CIO, Elliott Schlanger. A second benefit, he said, is that "The ITB members have somewhat of a vested interest in the success of implementing IT. These department heads are the men and women, who need to get things done. So, they provide active direction, as well as the strategic direction."

Maryland, Kansas, North Carolina, and other states have sensibly enough included private sector members—many of whom are corporate CIOs—on their advisory boards. The benefits here are pretty obvious: for one thing, it brings in a knowledge base that may be different from that of public servants. In addition, when it comes time for public-private partnerships—commonplace on such projects as fiber-optic networks—there's a greater ease in getting support for the effort from men and women who don't spend their lives in city hall or the statehouse.

In fact, some places maintain a board that goes beyond simple consultative authority; it's actually the final arbiter of IT decisions, with the CIO reporting to it. In Indianapolis, for example, the CIO reports to a city/county information technology board. This board is made up of mayoral appointees, county elected officials, county officials, and a judicial representative. While the mayor doesn't have the majority, his three appointees give him a fair amount of control.

This board actually approves all contracts of more than $25,000 (a crucial piece of power in a city that has outsourced many of its IT services). It approves the city's wide area network strategies as well. Boards such as the one in Indianapolis may not add value to the technical decisions. But they ensure the decisions appear fair and equitable.

Such an assumption of equity is of particular importance when it comes to questions of standards. If a city's health department is deeply invested in one kind of data collection software, and its corrections department has another, both have to feel they're being treated fairly when the central office makes a final decision as to which shall be the prevailing standard.

For far more about efforts to standardize technology, just move onto the next chapter.

In Summary

♦ As cities and states come to understand the importance of central authority—as discussed in the previous chapter—a leadership position, generally a chief information officer (CIO) is increasingly prevalent.

♦ A clear correlation was found between the existence of a CIO's job and good management in other areas covered by the Government Performance Project

♦ Typically, successful CIOs should ensure agencies are accountable to central guidelines; coordinate the efforts of agencies; reduce redundant efforts; help develop standards; and act as a conduit between the primary executive branch authority and the rest of government, with regards to IT.

♦ CIOs should not also be chief operating officers for day-to-day information technology needs; their job should be strategic in nature.

♦ Though many CIOs originate in technological positions, it's crucial that the officeholder be well acquainted with the overall goals and initiatives of government and the ways in which IT fits into entity-wide business plans.

♦ CIOs fall in a variety of places in entities' leadership schemes, but, generally speaking, the higher in the pantheon of government executives, the better.

♦ The existence of a smart, powerful CIO isn't, however, a magic amulet that ensures well-managed information technology. In fact, the best CIOs consult frequently with stakeholders at all levels to formulate IT plans.

◆ So-called information technology boards, which gather advice and seek support from agency heads and other stakeholders, are powerful tools.

6

Standardization: They Walk Alike and Talk Alike

Of all the basic concepts to good IT management, standardization is one of the easiest to grasp. As Elliot Schlanger, Baltimore's CIO, explained, "Just think of a telephone. Wherever you go, and whomever you're calling, you pick it up and you get a dial tone. It feels the same everyplace."

That kind of simplicity of use is the Holy Grail for computer technology. But telephone technology has been developing for a hundred years or so; computer networks, e-mail, and desktops are considerably more recent innovations. Eventually, as information technology matures, and certain standards emerge as overwhelmingly dominant, it's possible that standardization will no longer be much of an issue.

For now, however, a carefully considered set of standards—generally accepted, and backed by some kind of strong central enforcement—is a must-have for any government that wants to avoid wasting time and money.

Virtually every large city and state in the United States either has standards in place or is moving in that direction. In fact, when the expert advisory committee for the Government Performance Project met, the need for standards in IT software and hardware was an issue that required no debate. There was immediate consensus that this was a fundamental need for a well-managed city or state. Further, in interviews with central IT officials in the eighty-five entities covered by the GPP, not a single one argued against the idea of standardization in IT. The government officials did, however, cite a number of obstacles that stand in its way; some of which will be detailed later in this chapter.

Enterprise Architecture

Actually, a growing number of state and city governments don't really talk about standards, per se, anymore. Instead, government officials talk about an enterprise architecture that gives agencies somewhat more latitude to make their own purchasing decisions as long as they fit into a broad set of requirements. This is based on the logic that it probably doesn't matter a great deal whether an agency buys Dell or Gateway computers, as long as they can communicate with one another and use the same software effectively.

In Nebraska, the state government considered establishing sharp standards for the use of electronic mail but came to the conclusion that this wasn't really necessary. Instead, the state decided to standardize a small number of software packages that represented reasonable technology choices; so if a state agency used one of the four approved packages—each of which communicates easily with the other three—there would be no problem. "That approach avoided the religious wars that might have come if we required any single standard," said one high-level official.

In Kansas, gaining acceptance of an enterprise-wide IT architecture, which is based on standards, is a challenge the state is confronting head on. State officials talk about "leaving the road wide enough," to permit agencies to make intelligent selections, but narrow enough to make sure that no one deviates dramatically from the overall architecture.

A network can be a powerful tool in driving agencies toward standards. An agency that wants to use the city network had better purchase compatible equipment, warned Los Angeles's chief administrative analyst Jim House. "Agencies have a certain amount of capacity to buy things off the shelf, that may not be consistent. But one of the ways we promote standardization is if you want to attach to the network backbone, there are standards you have to comply with to do so."

A Range of Efforts

Right now, cities and states vary greatly in how far along they are in trying to achieve an integrated architecture. Some cities, such as Phoenix, have standardized virtually every crucial area of information technology. San Antonio, too, has become a leader in this area by making the sharing of information between city departments as well as between city and county agencies a fully accepted, completely automated practice. One benefit, for example, is that the San Antonio police department can do a wanted-person inquiry that can be matched against the city's municipal court database, the county's criminal justice database, and the state and national criminal databases.

Elsewhere in the country, things are somewhat less well coordinated. One Nashville official complained that the city has built "a huge computer network, piece by piece, without much of an idea of what it should look like when finished." Dallas, meanwhile, has had different local area networks for its police, city attorney, fire department, and water department. And though the city is trying to resolve the network conflicts, there are scores of different variations in the use of desktop software as well.

Even cities and states that are generally well run from an IT perspective have holes in their architecture. Philadelphia, for example, employs old technology in managing its prisons that doesn't easily interface with anything else in the city. As a result, the city has had to fund a separate data center to make information from its corrections department available elsewhere. In Iowa, as recently as 1999, the Department of Transportation e-mail system wasn't fully compatible with that in the rest of the state. One large problem with the system was that it couldn't accept e-mail attachments. As a result when the budget office had to send a document to the Department of Transportation, it had to be faxed (ironically, barely a decade ago, fax machines were the newest hot technology).

Generally speaking, the vast majority of states and large cities long ago saw the need for standards in telecommunications, and so there are relatively few problems there. Many have also moved forward—though there are still a fair number of exceptions—toward truly integrated networks. The biggest IT trouble spots that remain are conflicts in the hardware and software used in both government-wide systems, such as personnel, and those systems used at the agency level.

Why Standardize?

The most obvious problem with not standardizing across departments is that information can't be effectively shared. Horror stories abound about cities and states that can't even easily tell how many sick days their employees took in a year without dipping into two or three separate databases. Until recently, Washington, D.C., couldn't even reliably determine how many employees it had altogether.

Then there are missed efficiencies that can be gained when computers easily share data. In Massachusetts, for example, about half of the state's total budget is spent on human services. Unfortunately, a number of the agencies that provide help to the state's citizens have large computer systems precluded from communicating effectively with other agencies. Take case management, for example. The officials who run the state's welfare system, children's services, and Medicaid are all dealing with many of the same clients. But they're all working with stand-alone systems. As one official complained, "It sure would be nice if we had one case management system and everybody looked to that."

Of course, difficulties in accessing information and communicating are just the most obvious ones that emanate from using an unwieldy conglomeration of microchips. But there are a number of other issues that aren't so immediately apparent—especially to legislators who may not want to appropriate the necessary bucks to fully standardize. These difficulties in not standardizing include the following:

◆ **Double entering of data.** In Virginia Beach, for example, various agencies dealt with shortcomings in the city's entity-wide systems by building their own. One problem the city discovered was that this required time-consuming efforts to enter the same data into a variety of different systems. Even then, the city ran the risk that the different systems would wind up with different databases, out of synch with one another.

◆ **A strain on training.** It doesn't take a Harvard MBA to see that the more software systems that are in place, the more complex—and expensive—the training process is going to be. As one official in Michigan explained a couple of years ago, "Right now, we have to offer three levels of training in Word, three levels in Word Perfect, three levels in Excel, three levels in a variety of other systems, because there are still people using them."

◆ **Dead-end employees.** A corollary to the training issue is that it is difficult to transfer people from agency to agency or department to department if this requires retraining them on a new kind of technology. "One of the things we saw," explained Ivan Drinks, director of the IT Department in Denver, "was that because we had so many different systems, if we had people in one area, they couldn't be used in another."

◆ **Maintenance and support.** Given a shortage of qualified employees, most IT departments have difficulties keeping up with user needs even in the best-run governments. But when there are a score of different systems at work, maintaining a help desk, with sufficiently qualified personnel becomes a near impossibility.

Obstacles to Standardization

When formerly disorganized governments bring in new CIOs, often the first task on their desk is to make sure that all new purchases work together effectively and efficiently. But getting a state, city, or county's technology completely standardized isn't easy. As Michigan's CIO George Boersma said, "In a perfect world, you'd want a single system and all common data elements. I don't think there's a state, or business in the country that has that."

Part of the reason cities and states have found themselves burdened with nonstandardized equipment has been lack of foresight. But sometimes the fault lies in the governments' stars, not themselves. Occasionally, for example, cities and states are forced to use a particular piece of software in order to qualify for grants from higher levels of government. Cleveland, for instance, generally uses Microsoft products, but the Ohio Department of Health required the Health Department to submit reports by using a different software, Word

Perfect. "Well, the state gives us a lot of money, I'll let one Word Perfect hang around," said one official there.

Even more significantly, the speed with which technology has advanced has made the selection of standards a difficult and precarious process. Even the state or city with the most foresight in the world takes a risk that the equipment it buys in 2000 won't fit in with the advances available in 2005.

San Francisco, for example, saw the advantages to standardization long before many other cities. Yet today, it's a laggard in this area. Why? Because it was spooked by its decision in the 1980s to buy every IT product used by the city from Wang. Sounded good back then. But, as one official comments now, "When Wang started to die, we were stuck with all this old crap."

San Francisco is one of very few cities that hasn't been moving resolutely forward on developing and implementing standards. But a number of other cities and states cite a fear of being stuck with bad decisions as a reason they have moved slowly to adopt standards. And that's not the only obstacle. Here are several more:

◆ **Decentralization and autonomous agencies.** As one jaded CIO explained, "the vendor comes in, and the agency people get all starry-eyed." Of course, the more power that agencies have, the greater their capacity to ignore the suggestions or demands of a central IT office.

   Florida's agencies enjoy a fair amount of autonomy in how they approach their jobs. In fact, Florida has statewide constitutionally elected officers on the cabinet who are effectively peers with the governor in terms of their authority. So, if the legislature gives them the money to buy a system—whether or not it fits in with those found in the rest of the state—there's no one to stop them. In the words of one IT official, "They don't want to deal with someone telling them to use Lotus Notes."

   Similarly, as Los Angeles tries to standardize, it has to overcome the fact that its airport, harbor, water and power, and retirement systems, and to some extent its library and recreation and parks departments, have boards that can act independently. That gives them a certain amount of latitude to go their own way in making standardization decisions. "In some instances, the departments have a desire to proceed with something, and sometimes the short-term benefits outweigh the perceived benefits from architectural standardization," said one official. "That might take longer and cost more."

◆ **Overzealous standards.** The most successful standards are those that leave a certain amount of autonomy to the agencies, and that are regularly updated to keep in line with new advances. Richard Saig, former chief of information technology in Jacksonville, explained, "We have in the past said, here is the dictate. It won't be any other way. And when you get into those modes, you create more problems than you solve." In Delaware, it's made clear that the standards include "wiggle room" to permit innovation. The standards don't stultify bright managers from using their intellects; it informs their decisions so that they don't just go in foolish directions.

◆ **The difficulty of dealing with the old technology.** All the best-written standards in the world won't instantly remake the information technology of a state or city. It takes years for budgets to permit upgrading and changing the installed base of equipment to conform. Missouri's Mike Benzen explained, "We put together a subgroup task force for architectural standards. We cannot upgrade thirty different systems. They came back with standards. Anything new has to conform. We're living with lots of legacy systems. I am tied to an awful lot of legacy systems. There are tools that will allow almost anything to talk to anything. The problem is that it's expensive to do it."

Keys to Effective Standardization

With these obstacles in mind, there are a number of key thoughts that a city or state should keep in mind as it attempts to move toward standardization. The first step, of course, is clearly defining the standards that are going to be followed. Of course, any strategic plan that includes standards has to be updated on an ongoing basis. All effective CIOs must continually evaluate new technologies that may make old standards obsolete; because given two years without review, almost any thorough set of standards will be obsolete. In Minneapolis, leaders have an architecture meeting every Wednesday for a couple of hours, and as one official reported, "We constantly keep challenging ourselves."

This process of standardization will be most effective if it's done in collaboration with the agencies that are involved. Managers and end-users get very attached to the technology they're using. Unless they are persuaded that a change is genuinely in their self-interest, they're going to resist. Of course, overcoming the tendency among some governmental managers to create and defend fiefdoms is a matter of making sure they feel they were part of making the decision in the first place. (See Chapter 4.)

In Indianapolis, for example, the IT governance structure involves every city/county agency and department. Representatives meet on a regular basis in their own functional area—criminal justice or finance, for example—and they discuss changes to standards all the way down to what types of work stations are considered routine. Not long ago, the IT team in Indianapolis voted to stop using Dell computers as a standard PC configuration and to limit purchases to Hewlett Packard and Compaq. Once that decision was made, then no Dell computer could be bought, although the city continued to service old Dells.

In Phoenix, a thoroughly standardized city, the CIO is personally involved in working with each and every department to ensure they understand the logic behind the decisions being made. "We market it, so that they want to join, rather than making them," explained Danny Murphy, the city's CIO. What happens in Phoenix if someone still resists? "I say to the budget office, don't fund it. And it's not funded," Murphy said.

The reality is that even the best marketing job in the world won't necessarily elicit universal support from everyone affected by adopting a new IT system. When that is the case, more extreme measures, such as that described by Murphy, are then important. One official in Cleveland, for example, explained that for all city agencies funded by tax dollars, "We have published standards for desktop hardware and software and network hardware and software. The city used its Y2K effort to eliminate residual noncompliant software. The Division of Information Systems Services, which is our centralized IT function, establishes the standards and likewise they enforce them, with help from other folks. If I try and buy a piece of technology, and I just send my requisition to the purchasing department, purchasing won't approve it if it doesn't have an approval from Information Systems Services."

In Chicago, similarly, Business and Information Services strategic planners must approve all IT requests from departments. Strategic planners ensure that equipment and services being procured meet with the city's IT standards as outlined by the BIS architecture group.

Chicago, as with many other cities and states, doesn't only require agencies to comply: it makes sure that if they don't, they'll pay the price. Christopher O'Brien, director of management information services in Chicago, said: "The hammer is that we, the city's network and desktop support group, won't support anything that's not a city standard. I have kind of a mixed feeling; having us sign off on it does create a kind of bureaucracy. But until we get a culture here of adhering to standards, it's probably a necessary evil."

Virginia Beach's CIO David Sullivan echoed the same sentiments: "A major enforcement tool is ongoing support and maintenance. We only support those things that are standards."

Another powerful tool to encourage agencies to comply with standards are master contracts. The idea here is simple: if the central IT office makes a deal with a vendor to provide a certain product, quickly and easily and at a good price—and if the agency doesn't have to go through a complicated procurement process in order to buy that product—it's more likely than not that they'll follow along happily.

In Summary

◆ There's strong agreement among experts and practitioners that standardization of software and hardware is key to a well-managed city or state.
◆ There are a variety of benefits to standardization, including easy sharing of information; simplified data entry; savings on training; facilitating staff movement from job to job; and savings on maintenance and support.

◆ The reasons some cities and states are not sufficiently standard-ized include lack of foresight; the speed of change in technology; decentralization and autonomous agencies; bad experiences with too specific standards; and the cost of purchasing new tech-nology once standards are set.

◆ There's a relatively wide spectrum, among the cities and states, in terms of how completely standardized they are.

◆ Standardization does not have to mean extreme specificity in terms of the types of IT equipment purchased. Many well-managed entities refer instead to an entity-wide architecture, in which agencies are given a fair amount of freedom to select indi-vidual manufacturers, as long as their equipment ties into clearly stated standards.

◆ Some keys to effective standardization include regular reviews of standards to ensure an entity keeps pace with change; collabo-ration between the central IT office and the agencies in setting the standards; effectively marketing the utility of standards to agencies; central controls over procurement that force agencies to comply; and master contracts that make purchasing easier.

7

Strategic Planning: Getting from Here to There

In March 2000, *The Raleigh News Observer* in North Carolina trumpeted the disappointing news that the state was nine months behind on a major overhaul of its court computers. The $9.5 million project was part of an ambitious effort to automate the entire criminal justice system, but the project had been underfunded from its inception, and two years after installation began, court processes were still paper-intensive and two-thirds of magistrate's computers around the state hadn't yet been linked. What's more, the project was suffering from a lack of staff to train personnel to use the technology. "The Administrative Office of the Courts itself hasn't done a very good job of planning its technology," one official told the newspaper.

In the complex world of IT, good planning is a necessity at all levels—to provide an entity-wide vision, to coordinate disparate efforts among agencies, to minimize technological redundancy, and to prioritize decision making in a world in which spending possibilities are endless and resources are limited.

There's no guarantee that better planning would have eliminated the problems with the North Carolina court system, but it's likely it would have diminished them.

Jim House, chief administrative analyst in Los Angeles, discussed the city's choice to hire a consultant to help develop an information systems strategic plan. "Ultimately, we need to have some kind of vision for what comes first. We get requests all the time—(for example,) for a fiber optic link for the major sewage treatment plants near the airport. Whether that's justifiable or not is dependent on the strategic uses for that kind of information. You're talking about ripping up the streets for 15 or 20 miles for something that will only serve a fraction of the city. So, the question is why are we doing this? Is there some strategic reason why we need that kind of bandwidth and we need to do that? You'd find that budget requests would be more favorably received if they tied in with a strategic plan—an ability to articulate the benefits of certain budgetary initiatives."

False Efforts at Strategic Planning

House's comments are abundantly sensible, and yet in large cities and many states around the country, many government efforts get lumped under the terms of strategic planning, even when the actual activity has very little to do with either strategy or planning. Some government reports are simply snapshots of where an entity is, with very little thought about the future. Others are weighty tomes that aren't designed to actually be used; they turn into what one manager calls "credenza-ware."

In other instances, cities and states claim to have a strategic plan when all they really have is a vision of where the government wants to be at a certain point in the future. Certainly, such a "vision statement," is an essential part of a strategic plan, but it's only the beginning. Stopping with only a vision statement is like planning to build a house with a picture from *House Beautiful* and no blueprints.

At the other extreme, some governments argue that they have strategic plans when all they really have are detailed shopping lists of the items they intend to purchase; with no connection between them and a vision, goals, or objectives. This kind of document is properly called a "tactical plan." However, stopping with only a tactical plan—to continue the metaphor—is like trying to build a house by ordering all the materials, with no picture of the end-result.

When the Government Performance Project evaluated strategic planning in the cities and states, not only did reporters ask whether the entity actually had such a plan; they also checked with officials throughout government to see whether the plans were actually employed. Entities with a plan got a higher score than those without one; but for high grades, it was vital that the plans be used for practical applications on a regular basis. In fact, one manager facetiously suggested that the GPP follow something he called the "coffee-stain index" for evaluations, on the theory that the more coffee stains found on the actual printout of a strategic plan, the more it's being used.

What Should a Strategic Plan Contain?

Beyond the broad vision for the entity's IT, a genuine strategic plan should include specific long- and short-term goals; measures of progress toward reaching those goals; even more specific objectives that are required to reach the goals (here's where a tactical plan may tie into a strategic plan); clear assignment of responsibility for the achievement of those objectives; and, ideally, some discussion of potential obstacles and how they'll be dealt with. In the final analysis a good strategic plan looks at the government as a whole—focusing in on its operational needs and how the technology will satisfy them.

In fact, the best IT strategic plans are often found in cities and states that have a solid vision for the entity as a whole. Then, the IT plan can fit neatly into that broader perspective. "The fact that we have a real live strategic business plan makes it a lot easier to do a strategic IT plan," said Virginia Beach CIO David Sullivan. He pointed out that the fact that IT leaders participate in the development of the citywide plan for business operations makes them aware of what expectations there are for different operating agencies, as well as the outcomes they're trying to achieve. "We're rarely surprised by an initiative," he said. "We have systems analysts who work with almost every agency."

Enterprise-wide and Agency Plans

Up until this point, we've focused on enterprise-wide IT plans. In the best of all worlds, many individual agencies are preparing their own IT plans as well. The more reliant a particular agency is on technology, the more important it is for it to have its own plan. The elements that make for a good agency-wide plan are similar to those for the government as a whole. There can then be a back-and-forth interplay between agency plans and city or statewide ones.

The ideal for this exchange between agency and city, or agency and state, is to allow agencies to benefit from the common vision of the major entity, while making that entity's overall plan less authoritarian and more inclusive. Gary Langhoff, former budget director in Milwaukee, agreed, "I'm not only hoping but expecting that the new strategic plan will be much broader. It's going to be important for the CIO to understand that he or she is creating a plan not just for his or her own organization, but for systems citywide."

What's more, when agencies develop their own strategic plans, which are then incorporated in an enterprise-wide plan, all kinds of synergies may make themselves evident. If, for example, several city agencies plan to purchase imaging equipment over the course of the next several years, it's clear that the city would be well-advised to consider planning for ways to allow these agencies to share equipment.

Obstacles to Strategic Planning

As with most useful managerial devices, good strategic plans aren't easy to develop. One obvious problem is that they require a willingness to put in a fair amount of time and effort. Many government managers operate with insufficient resources, and they complain that they're far too busy dealing with the disaster of the day to spend a great deal of thoughtful time ruminating about how to avoid the disasters that are five years away.

In fact, 1999 may have been one of the low points for cities and states that wanted to concentrate on strategic planning. For many of them, the specter of the Y2K computer bug diverted resources that otherwise would have gone into this planning. It's hard to blame people for ignoring managing for the future, when the present seemed so threatening. But the best-managed cities and states seemed, somehow, to keep the strategic planning process going—even while they were trying to make sure that the water kept running on New Year's Eve.

Once strategic planning has been sufficiently institutionalized, the time savings it creates more than outweigh the time it actually takes. Other barriers, however, are more difficult to overcome.

The biggest problem is also the most obvious. How can you plan long-term in a field where change is constant? The city of Boston experienced firsthand the potential pitfalls implicit in this question. Several years ago, the city contracted with a consulting firm to set up an enterprise-wide strategic plan. When the plan was very late in its final delivery, the information it contained was dated and didn't reflect the current state of the IT department or new thoughts about where it wanted to go. The city, meanwhile, had spent a lot of staff time on interviews and other exercises to gather all the data together for the plan. Disappointed with a strategic plan that was substantially obsolete by implementation time, the city has no great desire to move in such a direction again.

Of course, Boston's experience was extreme—similar to someone who refuses to eat any vegetables after once choking on a piece of broccoli. But, generally speaking, real long-term planning is, at best, difficult. As one CIO pointed out, "Five years ago, we didn't even have a job classification for Webmaster." That doesn't mean that long-term planning isn't useful, of course. It simply means that it's most effective dealing with broad directions.

It makes sense in strategic planning to devise specific, procurement-oriented plans that only extend out as far as a year or two. In the years beyond that, the planning should be more general in nature, including some specifics, but focusing more on long-term projects, such as the establishment of a network, or the procurement of a major new piece of technology, such as an enterprise-wide financial management system. When you go beyond that, according to George Boersma, CIO of Michigan, "it better be high level."

Another problem is that the best-laid strategic plans are often mucked up by short-term political whims. After all, even the best-constructed strategic plans are only as powerful as their ability to persuade politicians to go along with them. An IT manager in Houston complained, "At one time, we did have a lot of plans in place. But we have a strong mayor type of government. And as new administrations come in there are new focuses, new initiatives, and basically some of the things that were put into place and planned have been put on hold."

This phenomenon is potentially most difficult where there's a great deal of turnover in leadership. As San Francisco's clear-talking comptroller Ed Harrington said, "Planning for almost everything is hard when you have term limits."

The Importance of Buy-in

There will never be a strategic plan so powerful that it can overcome extreme political will. But one safeguard in creating a strategic plan is to get sufficient buy-in to the planning process from as many people involved as possible. If the legislative and executive branches are both in tune with a plan, for instance, then a new mayor or a new body of legislators will find it somewhat more difficult to ignore. In Philadelphia, for example, the city has a very good strategic planning process in place, but one official complained that political considerations sometimes overrule sensible planning. To fix that, the city's CIO strongly recommended that Philadelphia create a central steering committee for IT, in hopes that decisions backed by general consensus would be immune to outside pressures.

Finally, strategic planning for IT cannot exist in a vacuum. In cities and states in which strategic planning is a relatively new—or even alien—concept, IT strategic plans are starting at a huge deficit. In Kansas City, the current strategic business plan covers two to three years for large-scale technology initiatives and the immediate business year for smaller initiatives. But as one IT source there said: "We don't have one business plan for the entire city. And without that, it makes it difficult to have an IT strategic plan that's in line with that one."

One of the biggest problems for Seattle in formulating its so-called IT Agenda was that the city as a whole didn't have a business plan. Seattle is now trying to structure things in a way that's more oriented toward using a business plan. "We hope that will drive future versions of the IT Agenda," said one city manager, "so it will be more like your traditional strategic plan."

Keys to Successful Strategic Planning

Some of these obstacles to successful strategic planning are out of the hands of the managers who are making them. But there are four general rules, which are generally followed by cities and states that use strategic planning successfully.

1. Updating Plans Regularly

Government plans need to be dynamic documents that reflect changing priorities—"evolving documents that allow for change," said one IT official from San Antonio. At minimum, long-range plans should be updated annually and supplemented by other shorter-term planning.

Taking the time to do the updating is extremely important, although sometimes the pressures of running a government get in the way. As Nashville's Richard McKinney said: "It's fine to think down the road, but you'd better keep yourselves on the road, as you're looking down it."

In fact, it's typical for governments to have good intentions in this area, but to slip. When interviewed in fall 1999, Baltimore officials were running about six months behind on the first update of their strategic information technology plan. "We're late. There's no excuse. We're late," said Elliot Schlanger, Baltimore's CIO.

In Denver, agency-specific plans that were last updated in 1998 had still not been updated at the end of 1999, even though an annual update was theoretically required. Due to Y2K and the implementation of some major new enterprise-wide systems, a decision was made to wait until 2000.

However, without updating, even plans that go out only a few years are soon as obsolete as an original IBM PC. At the extreme is

Hawaii, which has had an IT plan since 1988 and a requirement that each department is expected to prepare and update an annual plan. "But we don't have any people so we can't enforce it," said one IT manager. "Every year we get dinged for that in the third-party audit—we're not enforcing proper planning."

2. Getting Plenty of Input

The need of getting input from many players is explained by Earl Norton, data processing manager in the auditor's office in Arkansas. "The planning process used to be a top-down type of thing: 'This is what we want to do and this is how we intend to do it and you guys should follow along.' But with the proliferation of the knowledge of technology, now they have user groups that are really functional and meaningful toward setting direction of the plans."

In Baltimore, the Strategic Information Technology Plan, which represents both the government-wide and agency-specific requirements, covers a three-to-five-year planning horizon. The plan was generated with the input and guidance of the external business world, which is regarded as a big plus by IT managers. Similarly, in Chicago, the five-year strategic planning effort is quite strong and relies on input from an IT steering committee, including representatives from every city department. (The plan is then reviewed and approved by the mayor.)

In Minneapolis, the city uses a technology steering committee, composed of city department heads to create its enterprise information management structure. The steering committee's charter is to ensure that IT investments are aligned with citywide goals. CIO Don Saelens commented, "It's as good as I've ever experienced, in the private sector as well. And it's very inclusive—about 150 to 160 people are involved."

3. Linking the Strategic Plan and the Budget Process

This is a golden rule, as in, the person who has the gold, makes the rules. The more thoroughly the strategic plan can be incorporated in the budgetary process, the less likely it is that the obstacles described above will genuinely damage the integrity of the plan.

In Minnesota, for example, agencies were required to associate their budgetary requests with a component of strategy in the master plan. Thus, as the state reviews budget requests, they are focused on the strategy within the IT master plan that supports that request. Chicago maintains a five-year information technology plan, but conducts annual planning sessions that coincide with the budgeting process. Milwaukee also has a citywide strategic information plan and incorporates IT planning as part of the annual budget process. Strategic and tactical level plans are developed and adopted by departments in conjunction with the budget.

In Phoenix, the city has a ten-year architecture vision, updated annually. The Information Technology Department meets with each department and a representative of the budget and research office to discuss the agency's IT plan and its budget request. The meetings allow the department an opportunity to highlight their departmental technology priorities. After the meetings, ITD ranks each budget request based on citywide and departmental technology priorities on a three-point scale (essential to dispensable). The budget request report is updated with ITD rankings and returned to Budget and Research.

4. Integrating IT Planning into Other Business Plans and Vice Versa

If IT planning is not incorporated into other city or state plans, the likelihood of the IT plan succeeding declines. Just as enterprise-wide plans generally refer to personnel issues (at minimum asking how much it will cost to staff a new project), they should also intersect repeatedly with IT plans. In Florida, for example, there's a requirement that when agencies do their overall business plans, they must include technology issues in them.

Conversely, in Hawaii, one problem with planning is that strategic business planning and IT planning have been conducted independently. "With no direct participation in making strategic business decisions, IT planning can only be reactive and opportunities for creative application of IT may be lost," one state manager explained.

In Summary

◆ Cities and states need to develop strategic plans in order to guide their future efforts in information technology.

- Many entities that recognize the need for strategic planning have efforts that don't provide sufficient utility. These include plans with a vision for the future, but no counsel on how to reach that vision, or little more than a shopping list of planned procurements (a "tactical plan").
- Ultimately, for a strategic plan to be successful, it has to actually be used by managers at all levels.
- A good strategic plan should contain specific long- and short-term goals; measures of progress toward reaching those goals; even more specific objectives that are required to reach the goals; clear assignment of responsibility for the achievement of those objectives; and, ideally, some discussion of potential obstacles and how they'll be managed.
- Ideally, a good strategic plan for IT fits in with an entity-wide strategic plan that drives toward city or statewide goals.
- Agencies that are IT dependent should also develop their own strategic plans—which fit in with the entity-wide IT plan.
- Among the major obstacles to strategic planning are the amount of time required to do the job properly; the fast-changing nature of IT; and political whims that may value popular short-term objectives over longer-term benefits.
- Successful strategic plans are not top-down efforts but get buy-in from the agencies themselves.
- Among the keys to successful strategic planning are updating plans regularly; getting a great deal of input from stakeholders; and linking the strategic plan and the budget process and integrating IT plans with other business plans for the entity.

8

Procurement:
Buy Buy Buy

The procurement function in government is enormously important. Both taxpayers and government employees benefit when governments get the most value out of the money spent on supplies and equipment, both small and large. Value, of course, is more than just getting the cheapest deal available. Procurement value also implies purchasing a product that will do the job effectively and efficiently.

However, government purchases are not always this successful. Approval processes for government purchasing, rules for equitable bidding, and controls on the procurement process have been set up over decades to protect governments from corruption, favoritism, and just plain thoughtless purchasing.

Nobody can argue with those goals, but the controls put into place to safeguard procurement have tended to prolong the process dramatically. This, of course, is not much of a problem when someone is waiting for office furniture, for example. Your old desk chair may squeak and may have a rip in its upholstery, but that squeak and unsightly tear won't really impede your productivity. Information technology is a vastly different story. From coast to coast, there's a tension between standard procurement processes and speedy purchase of technology.

One extreme example is in West Virginia. Over the years, that state had a series of unfortunate incidents involving fraud on the part of state officials. Understandably, the state took steps to ensure that procurement could not be completed without a number of checks and balances. This is all well and good, but now it takes the state many, many months to make a major procurement. "It can be a real pain," said one IT official there.

In fact, in West Virginia, the legislation holds the state purchasing director or agency head personally liable for any purchasing foul-ups. "Hell," commented the IT official, "you're putting your house on the line for all practical purposes." Given this high level of personal responsibility, it's a wonder that West Virginia managers aren't using abacuses.

Delays Are Destructive

Curiously, many state and city governments do not seem to have effectively caught on to the idea that IT procurement is a whole new kind of beast, in which speed of purchase is of paramount importance. In the rapidly changing technological world, the problems caused by delay are obvious. A technology manager in Iowa complained that until new legislation was passed on April 25, 2000, his state was confronted with a host of problems caused by making purchases on a government schedule. "If generationally, IT changes every 15 months and I have to submit a budget on October 1 of one year and we get the money the following July, by the time we go through notification and justification, I'm a generation behind."

"We didn't have any performance measure set for turnaround time," added one Indianapolis IT authority. "So other service levels that were identified got top priority."

Decentralized Purchasing

One frequently suggested solution to tardy government purchasing is freeing agencies from many of the shackles of centralized controls. This freedom can be effective—to a point. The process for selecting a vendor for a new financial system in Seattle took about one third the time it had for the prior, similar system. What happened? "We've allowed more authority to go out to the departments," said an official there. "Up to a certain range, departments can do their own request for proposal (RFP) process, with some consultation from purchasing. And that's helped quite a bit in speeding it up. How fast it actually happens, depends on the departments' ability to put the stuff together and do the evaluation."

Unquestionably, freeing agencies to do their own purchasing for commodity items is a good idea. The use of master contracts, about which more information will follow, also eases those projects dramatically.

But when it comes to bigger, more complicated procurements, decentralization of purchasing can open up a Pandora's desktop of problems. In Alabama, which has traditionally been a very decentralized state, CIO Eugene Akers discussed the problems: "We have vendors going out and convincing small agencies to jump on the client server bandwagon. They have no idea of the cost of ownership or the fact that the state has no skill set. They get in cheap on the front end, and then they have a problem. I have been kicking back contracts to agencies over the last couple of months, telling them I'm not going to approve it until I see a five-year plan. A lot of them aren't even getting warrantees or maintenance contracts. They're getting sold on the idea that they can make the purchase for [very little] and then they'll worry about it down the road."

All of this leads to lesson number one in expediting procurement of IT: agencies should earn greater authority to make procurements by demonstrating that they have the skill to do so without mucking up.

Requests for Proposal (RFP)

Central oversight to monitor agencies' purchasing skills is vital. Perhaps the most important capability—all too often lacking in government agencies—is being able to put together a well-researched, well-thought-out request for proposal (RFP).

One of the most significant problems in writing an RFP is that too little time is spent before the actual document is submitted. To create a truly useful RFP, agencies must first think through precisely what it is they want their new purchase to accomplish. Without such advance planning, problems frequently ensue. A common case occurs when committees of potential users each throw in their thoughts on the subject, and then some unfortunate project manager is assigned the task of patching it all together in some kind of sensible document. To paraphrase the well-worn cliché, a badly thought out RFP for a horse, may well mean that an agency winds up buying a camel. Or else it has to change its camel-oriented RFP a few times before it comes close to actually describing a thoroughbred.

As one IT manager in San Antonio explained, "A big problem is lack of sufficient preparation in the departments, which may go through two or three RFP's before they really figure out what they want and need."

This has certainly been a problem in Connecticut in years past. The time it took for that state to complete various projects sometimes stretched out years, largely because minimal planning had taken place. What often happened was that vendors would uncover weaknesses in the original RFP, and the state agency would have to go back in and document their requirements more carefully. That process was too often very time consuming.

One Los Angeles official complained about a similar situation: "A factor that can contribute to delays is a scope of work that is open for interpretation, resulting in dramatically different proposals. This requires staff to more carefully analyze the competing proposals and on occasion, may result in the proposals being rescinded."

So, you might say, the answer is a balance between agency authority and central oversight of the RFP process. But that just solves part of the problem. Central control only make sense when the central office knows what it's doing. There's no guarantee that traditional purchasing officials—accustomed to buying filing cabinets, cars, and carpeting—will be up to the task of overseeing the purchase of high-tech equipment, too.

Central Expertise

With that in mind, it's still often the case that the best controls include a fair amount of input from the central information technology office. Marlene Lockard, director of the Department of

Information Technology in Nevada described the process in her state, "We have within the department—our department—a contract administration section. It is responsible for technology RFPs. They're done here, rather than in the purchasing division. We have assembled a core team that's experienced at technology acquisitions. We're doing a better job."

External Obstacles

Sadly, even with a well-thought-out RFP, the process often takes far too long, thanks to a variety of factors that have been legislated over the years and are out of the hands of the agency or the IT office. For example:

◆ **Social policies and other restrictions.** In and of themselves, social policies tied to procurements are perfectly legitimate. There's no reason why a city or state shouldn't try to further various worthwhile agendas through purchasing policies. Unfortunately, these policies can slow things down dramatically—and cities and states would be well advised to balance the impact of tortoise-like IT procurements against the benefits achieved by pre-set conditions.

   In Los Angeles, for example, to buy from a vendor, the city must be assured that it doesn't do business in Myanmar (Burma), and it must prove it has a reasonable child care policy. In San Francisco, vendors working with the city must offer proper benefits to their employees. In Houston, vendors are required to adhere to the city's policies regarding drug testing indemnification and participation by minority and/or women-owned businesses. Houston also has an indemnification policy that "indicates that we even want you to insure us, in case we screw up and we hurt ourselves," explained one manager there. "And most of the vendors take exception to that. So, we have to negotiate on that particular issue. And usually they win. But it slows things down."

◆ **Low thresholds for formal processes and approvals.** In New Hampshire, the CIO must personally approve specific requests greater than $5,000. In Iowa in 1999, an RFP was required if an item was not on contract and the expenditure was greater than $5,000. The result in Iowa was a really unpleasant boomerang: "We overbuy when we get a chance to buy," one manager admitted. "Then it's tired iron."

◆ **Vendor holdups.** Mississippi has a careful process for issuing an RFP that includes advertising it twice, waiting thirty days for responses, and then going through a reasonably complicated evaluation process. But that is not the end of the state RFP process. If vendors think something unfair has occurred, they can protest—and that can hold up action for another three to six months.

Of course, these issues are troublesome in that they slow down the process. Other governments grapple with legislative problems that make it difficult for them to get the right equipment under any circumstances. Most troublesome are those public sector entities that continue to require that the low bid be taken; regardless what other factors may be involved. Alabama's CIO criticized this stipulation, "You cannot get around low bid. And believe me we've brought this up a few times to state purchasing; but they're attached to it." Why? "There's less grief, it keeps them out of jail."

Master Contracts

Fortunately, from coast to coast, cities and states have discovered that one good way to avoid a lengthy RFP process is to avoid an RFP altogether. This is, as mentioned above, most easily accomplished with so-called commodity items; those that the city or state is buying with some frequency.

With commodity items, states and cities can devise master contracts (also called blanket contracts and price agreements). The idea here is simple. The state or city comes up with an RFP for a commodity item—desktop computers, for example—which it puts out in the marketplace. A number of vendors put in bids, and the entity selects one or more that are acceptable in both quality and price. Then, if an agency within the entity has the money, and needs one of these commodity items, it can simply purchase from the preapproved list.

In many cities and states as much as 90 percent or more of commodity purchases are handled through master contracts. Master contracts not only shortcut the long and arduous procurement process, but they help support standards, since only approved hardware and software are made available.

George Boersma, CIO in Michigan, explained: "We looked at procurement and said, 'what are we doing here?' About 80 percent of the transactions were under $1,000 representing about 20 percent of the volume. So we were aggressive in putting together procurement contracts. We said, 'lets get the paperwork out.'"

Master contract prices in Michigan and elsewhere are not set in stone. So, if the price of a desktop computer goes down, which they do frequently, "Our prices reflect it immediately," said Boersma. "And we have that information on the web. So our end user can go see the price of something and they know precisely what it is today."

Missouri's award-winning Prime Vendor initiative has taken the master contract effort about as far as any state. Missouri establishes a contract with a single vendor, which is required to carry six top-rated product lines. It negotiates for a purchase price that's six percent over the acquisition price; and includes service and maintenance among other things. The state could have gotten a price at four percent of acquisition, but it wanted to guarantee that the services it was demanding were top drawer. As a result, the agencies get a choice of many products, with a single point of contact, and a guaranteed high level of service.

Many cities—including Buffalo, Boston, Memphis, Milwaukee, New Orleans, and Phoenix—are able to hook into state-negotiated contracts. Both states and cities benefit in these instances, as they can negotiate better prices with larger potential purchases.

Washington has brought in both state government and localities very effectively with its so-called "E-Mall," at www.emall.dis.wa. gov. This on-line site resembles amazon.com more than it does the typical governmental Web site. At the E-Mall site, both state and local officials in Washington can purchase hardware and software from the state's master contracts, conveniently window-shopping through a variety of vendors whose wares have been approved.

Master contracts aren't limited to just hardware and software, either. They can extend to service contracts, as well, making it far easier for agencies to avail themselves of various consulting services. Mississippi, for instance, sends out an RFP on various classifications of consulting every six months. Then agencies can pick from the list of approved firms. What's more, "We ask them to negotiate for a lower price than that which was quoted," said one IT official there.

There is one warning here. While master contracts are a grand idea, there is room for potential problems with their overuse. Some governments have found themselves with so many master contracts in place that they begin to lose their natural efficiencies. As one observer remarked, "Once you've got seven or eight master contracts for one item, it's almost as if you don't have any."

This happened in Seattle. Dwight Dively, the city's finance director explained, "We might have had eight blanket contracts for PCs. Now, we want to have maybe one or two that provide for all of those things. So, we acquire much more systematically and coherently; it's an evolution of what we've done."

Other Innovations

Okay so master contracts can help grease the runways for commodity items. But what about those larger purchases that don't lend themselves to mass purchases? Thankfully, there are a number of innovations that may help.

◆ **Competitive sealed proposals.** Delaware IT officials are permitted to accept a tentative price on an acquisition and negotiate to a conclusion, without need for a stringent RFP full of conditions and details. If the first vendor doesn't work out, in negotiations, the state can go on to its next choice; then its third. Similar modifications of the RFP process, in which negotiations ease the way, are being used in a number of other venues including Long Beach, California, and New York City. In Long Beach a charter amendment allowed the city to negotiate directly with vendors, as an alternative to rigid, document-based efforts. New York City is also doing negotiated acquisitions and "strongly discourages" the use of RFPs. No wonder. The process for moving an RFP forward in the nation's largest city requires a minimum fifty-four-day announcement in the city record, holding public hearings, registration with the Comptroller's Office (which has a maximum of thirty days to release funds), and clearance through the city's vendor approval system. Split funding, where funding must be drawn from both capital and operating budgets requires additional approvals and processing time.

◆ **Prequalified vendors.** This is a particularly common-sense approach where the state, or city, asks that vendors go through a fairly straightforward process before they even bid for RFPs. Nevada, Michigan, and other entities have shaved weeks off the process through this simple effort.

◆ **Cooperating with other governments.** Virginia Beach worked with its neighboring communities on a number of IT procurements in order to develop joint RFPs and joint contracts including IT professional staffing contracts and wireless cellular service contracts.

◆ **Letting the vendor do the work.** This is one of the most important keys to a successful RFP process. There's simply no point in a city or state limiting a vendor's options by a too specific design. Providing some flexibility allows vendors to provide creative solutions to a government's problems; without the government itself having to invest the time and money in research and development.

◆ **Using "technology refresh clauses."** Given the speed of change, this is one way to alter the nature of an original RFP, relatively painlessly. Listen to Alan Harbitter, chief technology officer at PEC Solutions, Inc., which designs, analyzes, and implements government information processing systems: "The RFP should contain provisions that permit the Government to quickly add new goods and services to the contract while retaining beneficial terms and conditions and discount levels throughout the technology refresh process. The alternative is to be forced into a situation where acquired goods and services are obsolete before they are deployed."

Twelve Guidelines for Dealing with Vendors

There are a number of other useful approaches to successfully working with vendors. Few people in the private sector are more articulate about these efforts than Bob Campbell, a principal and regional industry leader at Deloitte Consulting in Austin, Texas. Following are his twelve guidelines for making this crucial relationship a successful one.

1. Where feasible, elicit vender reactions to your procurement plans before the formal request for proposal is submitted. Vendors frequently have ideas concerning approaches to meeting your objectives that can be elicited during procurement planning. This may be accomplished through techniques such as informal meetings with individual vendors, interactive vendor forums, a procurement Web site with the facility for questions and answers, and the issuance of a draft offering document for vendor review and comment. This approach may have the residual benefit of increasing competition, as the vendors perceive a fair and open process.

2. Clearly establish your desired level of service from the vendor community up front—don't leave this to vendors to guess about. In the event the level of service affects both costs and the level of benefit received, the desired level of service should be specified. Depending on the procurement, the desired service level could include the desired timeliness, desired accuracy levels, frequency of service, numbers and qualifications of vendor personnel committed, and desired reporting levels. Inadequately defined service levels will lead to "apples and oranges" among vendors—and ultimately a disappointed buyer.

3. Provide full access to policies, procedures, current system documentation, and organization/staffing charts. (But be sure the information provided is current and accurate.) An informed vendor is able to prepare a more responsive proposal. Furthermore, full access to such information tends to encourage competition as no one has a particularly favored position based on prior knowledge or prior access to information.

4. Be sensible about contractual terms and conditions. The marketplace is changing. Many of the proven vendors are resource constrained and have choices. Deployment of "old school" procurement terms and conditions significantly discourages competition and frequently leads to protracted contract negotiation processes with the selected vendors. Some of the more contentious provisions can relate to: blanket indemnification provisions beyond personal injury and property damage; vendor liability for consequential damages in areas outside vendor control; unwillingness to provide an overall cap on vendor liability; and liquidated damage provisions that can "break the bank."

5. When creating performance incentives, make sure they are "two-sided." In other words, do not just create penalties for performance problems, but offer financial rewards for superior performance as well. This is only fair, and it serves to align buyer and vendor objectives.

6. Understand that you typically are not going to get something for nothing. Marked pricing differences among qualified major firms almost always reflect different understandings concerning scope and intentions to commit different resource levels to a project. This issue is fundamental to fair evaluation and vendor selection decisions, as well as ultimately achieving the buyer's objectives. Frequently the playing field can be leveled by specifying up front to all proposers the level of resources intended to be expended. This allows the evaluation to focus on capabilities and value for a specified constant amount rather that comparing "apples and oranges."

7. Allow a fair time for qualified vendors to prepare credible responses. Vendors frequently have multiple client commitments and proposals going on concurrently. That's business. Providing vendors with advance notice of planned procurements ahead of time helps. With that said, allowing at least two to three weeks for relatively simple straightforward proposals and at least four to six weeks for complex proposals is reasonable. Affording less time will compromise the level of competition and the quality of proposals received.

8. Verify vendor representations in the proposal evaluation process. Unfortunately, some vendors will stretch the truth in the interest of winning a proposal. It is important that verification be conducted during proposal evaluation, including reference checks for firm experience, reference checks for individual experience, review of products and/or prior deliverables, and review of financial statements.

9. Be careful not to equate the ability to write well with the ability to execute successfully. Many vendors have eloquent technical writers who can produce beautiful prose—whether or not the vendor has actual experience in doing what you desire. Nothing substitutes for a vendor having proven reference sites where the vendor has previously successfully performed what you are seeking to buy.

10. Get to know the key players who will represent the vendor in project delivery. Your confidence in these people and "chemistry" with your people is frequently an important ingredient of success. This may be accomplished through interviews of vendor senior executives and account managers during the proposal evaluation process. Don't hesitate to ask: am I comfortable that this person can deliver? Is this someone with whom I would want an ongoing professional relationship?

11. If you are going to ultimately be responsible for running the business processes and/or technology being implemented, get your operations staff involved from the start. This is basic change management. If your employees are not part of the development of the solution, they will likely resist it once it is implemented and laid on them.

12. Be sure that you believe a vendor can back up their commitments. From time to time, governments will vest large and mission critical assignments to organizations that lack the resources to meet their commitments. Be sure to determine during the proposal evaluation: What competing demands for vendor resources exist? What is the level of capitalization of the firm to back up commitments made?

In Summary

◆ The pressure to procure information technology in a timely and efficient fashion is paramount.

◆ Delays can be costly—and almost inevitably ensure that a government is working with old equipment.

◆ Unfortunately, there has developed a conflict between the need for speedy purchases, and reasonable desires to make sure the process is fair, honest, and equitable.

◆ Some decentralized purchasing can be effective, as long as adequate central controls are in place to ensure that the agencies have adequate resources to make sensible, compatible purchases.

◆ Possibly the most important step in skillful purchasing is the first one; creating a strong RFP, with a great deal of thought going into the front end—before the request goes out.

◆ Even with a solid RFP, and a well-run procurement system, other obstacles can slow down the process including social policies and other restrictions; low dollar thresholds for formal processes; inevitable vendor snafus; and legal restrictions such as unreasonable low-bid policies.

◆ One way to speed up the process—for commodity-type purchases, particularly—are master contracts, which allow an agency to buy off a preapproved list of items as long as they have the money.

◆ Some other procurement techniques that have been found useful include prequalified vendors; cooperating with other governments; technology refresh clauses; competitive sealed proposals; and efforts to create good vendor relationships.

◆ There are a number of ways to work effectively with vendors; a few that stand out include eliciting vendor reactions to proposals before a formal RFP is issued; clearly establishing required levels of service; providing full access to your entity's procurement policies; and ensuring that a vendor can back up its commitments.

9

Outsourcing

In the Government Performance Project's analysis of human resources, it became clear that the biggest single personnel problem for cities and states in the United States was a fast-growing shortage of trained technology workers. Of course, governments have long suffered shortages of various employees; certain types of teachers are often hard to find; engineers have periodically been in short supply and right now, it's tough to find a good librarian.

But it may well be the case that at no time has there ever been a shortage of a particular kind of employee coupled with such explosive growth in demand from both the public and private sectors. For example, although there has been a periodic paucity of science teachers, there's not a whole lot of private sector demand for people who can effectively teach mitosis to high school freshmen.

With a growing number of technology initiatives in the public sector, government entities have found themselves fiercely competing with corporations for the same technology talent. While many people who choose to work for cities and states do so for reasons other than the pay level, the public sector is at a disadvantage when it comes to compensation—a dominant factor in workers' decision who to work for. City hall can't give stock options, and city hall can't pay as much as well-heeled corporations, such as Microsoft or Oracle.

Christopher O'Brien, director of business and information systems in Chicago, explained the problem for the public sector: "We couldn't hire people at the salaries we needed. We saw that in an environment like this, with people being paid what they were being paid, we weren't going to be able to maintain the level of expertise that we needed."

So Chicago as well as a growing number of other cities and states are turning to "outsourcing," using private sector partners to fill their needs. The range of uses for outsourcing varies, of course, but it seems overwhelmingly likely to become increasingly popular over the coming years. Unfortunately, there hasn't been sufficient experience with the device in information technology to learn a great many lessons about what works and what doesn't. But for many of the cities and states that have taken the outsourcing route already, the initial reports are favorable.

Some Successful Outsourcing Efforts

Chicago for instance, outsourced support of its network and desktop services to IT giant Unisys. The arrangement appears successful, so far, based on preliminary customer satisfaction surveys. Chicago conducted a baseline customer survey about a year before its outsourcing effort began. Then it sent out another survey when the contract took hold in March 1999 and another in the summer. By summer, customers already were letting officials know there was an improvement. (Part of the outsourcing agreement requires regular customer satisfaction surveys.)

One city that has done substantial outsourcing is Indianapolis. In May 1995, the city selected the SCT Corporation to provide IT management services. SCT now provides data center management and support of the local as well as wide-area network; it supports the distributed computing environment including servers; it supports applications development and the maintenance effort; and it also provides technical support of the Internet and Web site. SCT does not provide the project management focus for the city's Web site or support public safety applications development. SCT also does not support the court system. But otherwise it does just about everything else. The planning function is done in collaboration with city/county staffers who have retained control of the contract.

As with Chicago, one reason Indianapolis took the outsourcing route was simply that the city's own Information Services Agency was running out of capacity to deal with all the city's technology issues. Another reason was that the city, as with just about all governments, was having a hard time holding on to the technology workers it could lure, at traditional government salaries.

Why not raise traditional government salaries for IT experts? This is not politically feasible according to Emily Duncan, former CIO for Indianapolis: "There was a lot of hesitation about introducing those high level salaries, because in many cases they'd be making more than the county prosecutor. So it was more palatable to outsource and pay them a lot more."

Some Lessons from Indianapolis

Obviously, Indianapolis has learned some interesting lessons in dealing with an outsourcing contract that is so comprehensive. The following are some insights picked up by Duncan on outsourcing:

◆ The city originally signed a seven-year outsourcing contract with fixed costs. In the future, she indicated, leaders will likely look at a shorter-term contract that offers more flexibility. It's been a challenge for the city to manage a seven-year contract with fixed costs in a way that enables the city/county to stay price competitive but doesn't affect service.

◆ In the future the city also might consider spreading an outsourcing contract around to several companies. "Having everything come from one vendor might not give you the ability to get the best price," she said. "But we had to do what we did to take that leap. To tiptoe into the icy cold water meant we'd never get in below our ankles. I think we've done a pretty good job."

◆ One of the biggest surprises was that change didn't come as quickly as expected. "You go into one of these contract negotiations and talk for six months about how fabulous everything is going to be. So, at the stroke of midnight, you sign the contract, hand over a big fat check; and there are all these new folks and you think, 'I'm so excited, it's like Christmas Eve,' and you're so excited about what's going to be there. And three months later, Santa still hasn't arrived."

A Half-way Approach to Outsourcing in San Diego

The city of San Diego has taken a slightly different approach to outsourcing that's worth considering. About twenty years ago, the city realized that its civil service system couldn't attract and retain good technical people. The city decided it could solve its problems by creating a separate nonprofit agency that was independent and could contract for IT services.

The result was the San Diego Data Processing Corporation—a city-owned, independent nonprofit corporation that sells a variety of IT services to the city via an operating agreement. The Data Processing Corporation uses its $80 million a year contract to provide some services directly, such as managing the city's network, while outsourcing others. It procures a wide range of services including even wire telecommunications.

One major advantage San Diego has discovered is that the IT process is far more streamlined than if it were part of the normal political process. Richard Wilkin, the city's information technology and communications director explained, "We don't have the pressures that you might get if the city itself was doing its procurements, in terms of [companies or individuals] lobbying officials during that process."

By and large, according to Wilken, San Diego officials are satisfied with the half-way arrangement, although some local managers would consider moving to true outsourcing, as Indianapolis has done. The big question in San Diego has been how to hold the Data Processing Corporation fully accountable. Wilkin elaborated, "If, for example, you've got a fixed-price contract on a project and you [spend far more than anticipated] who pays? Ninety-five percent of SDDPC's revenues come from the city. That creates challenges."

Meanwhile, the trend toward outsourcing continues to accelerate. San Diego County has issued a ten-year contract outsourcing its computer and telephone systems. About two-thirds of the county's $100 million IT budget falls under the contract. Pennsylvania has been in the process of outsourcing its data centers. And Memphis is at the early stages of outsourcing its entire IT operation, including its management.

Outsourcing Obstacles

Naturally, the road to outsourcing isn't always smooth. (In fact, it probably never is smooth; sometimes it's so rutted and potholed that a tire blows on the way there.) Iowa considered outsourcing, for example, but rejected it, deciding instead to streamline its current operations in order to accomplish the same goals. A few years ago, an outsourcing effort in Indiana ran into a major obstacle when the executive branch of the state made the mistake of moving forward without sufficient input from the legislature, the unions, and state technology workers. "When the decision was announced, it was a major shock to everyone's system," said the state's former CIO.

Perhaps the most dramatically failed effort to outsource occurred in Connecticut in the late 1990s. An outsourcing plan was set in motion in 1996 after a consultant's report found the state's computer systems to be seriously outdated and poorly run. The request for proposals was issued in February 1997, and the administration hoped to outsource the state's systems by mid-1997. "We shouldn't be in the business (of information technology)," proclaimed the state's governor, John Rowland.

But the process of selecting a vendor dragged on and on. And meanwhile, Connecticut's IT efforts were less than adequate, as the state awaited outsourcing assistance that would remedy their problems. In February 1999, the Government Performance Project described the state's IT management efforts this way: "It is a morass of disjointed systems with computers in one department unable to communicate with those in another. Information is fragmented and unnecessarily duplicated. There are at least a dozen e-mail systems, and many don't link up well with each other. Information technology has historically been poorly managed in Connecticut, and the state hasn't done a good job of procuring new systems. Nor is the security of the systems the best available. No one knows exactly how many computers the state owns."

Soon after that appraisal was released, the state finally completed the process of selecting a contractor from three major corporations. It chose Electronic Data Systems (EDS) for a seven-year outsourcing contract that was initially estimated at $1 billion. When an article on Connecticut's outsourcing effort appeared in *Governing* in June 1999, Rowland's administration was still in the process of negotiating final contract terms with EDS. But rumblings from the legislature about the proposal quickly grew to a fearsome pitch. "The House speaker was publicly expressing dissatisfaction with the information about the plan that she was getting from the CIO," the magazine reported.

Other problems cited in the article: "Opponents say they worry about turning the technology so many state agencies depend on over to one prime contractor and about losing IT employees and the institutional memory they hold. They also say they don't understand how a company can promise better pay and benefits for Connecticut's IT workers and buy and install new and improved technology, while saving the state $50 million a year and making a profit. They also wonder if signing a seven-year contract so entwines the state with one vendor that it will be difficult to extricate itself from the contract if need be. They fear that if the state becomes so dependent on one vendor, that vendor could demand changes in contract prices or the services provided, and the state would have no alternative but to give in."

On June 29, 1999, Governor Rowland announced that he was canceling his plan to outsource the state's executive-branch information technology systems. Rowland's announcement came after the state's CIO informed him that, after months of negotiations, the state and EDS could not agree on the total cost of the project and what would be included in the base price of the contract. "This leads me to conclude that entering into an agreement with EDS on its terms is an unacceptable risk for the state to take," the CIO told the governor in a June 28 letter. Rowland said negotiations with another vendor considered for the outsourcing project, IBM Global Services, would not be reopened.

What lessons can be learned from Connecticut's humbling experience?

◆ Before it's possible to effectively outsource IT, or anything else, it's vital that a government entity really understand how much it's paying to deliver that service itself. It is no surprise that Indianapolis is a national leader in this kind of "activity-based costing," as it's called.

◆ Connecticut, like Indiana before it, discovered that an outsourcing effort simply won't get off the ground without buy-in from the major players as early in the process as possible.

◆ It would appear that cities and states that begin outsourcing in a small way tend to be more successful than those that want to take the plunge and turn over every last element of IT all at once. Even Indianapolis, as seen above, still maintains certain of its own IT functions.

◆ Implausible promises, such as those made in Connecticut, are likely to scare off skeptics, often justifiably.

◆ As Duncan in Indianapolis suggested, shorter-term contracts are likely to be far less risky; they leave the state less vulnerable to a contract that simply doesn't work out.

◆ As Duncan also pointed out, critics may be somewhat less fearful if a state doesn't turn everything over to one big contractor.

Outsource—But Keep Control

In general, the rules effecting privatizing computer operations are the same that apply to any major effort of this kind. And perhaps the most important of these is the following: cities and states can turn over a huge portion of the operational elements of their IT efforts. But they cannot turn over responsibility. The major planning and oversight must still reside within the government itself, not with the contractor. At the end of the day, no government can tell its citizens that an IT problem isn't its fault, regardless of who the city or state has hired to do the job.

As Barbara Jordan once said, "The stakes . . . are too high for government to be a spectator sport."

In Summary

◆ According to the GPP, the most prevalent problem in information technology is a shortage of qualified workers. One solution is to outsource IT efforts to private sector firms.

◆ It's still relatively early to judge many ongoing outsourcing efforts; but many of those studied in the GPP appeared to be reasonably successful.

◆ Indianapolis has been a leader in outsourcing (both in IT and other government areas). Two of the lessons learned in that state include the potential benefits of using multiple vendors and the fact that change does not come as rapidly as many expect.

◆ The city of San Diego has taken a slightly different path, using a hybrid called the San Diego Data Processing Corporation, which is set up with city money and runs as a quasi-independent authority.

◆ Successful outsourcing requires buy-in from the parties involved. In Connecticut, an effort to outsource all of the state's IT efforts was derailed, in part, because the executive branch had not gotten all the parties involved; in part because of lack of overall planning.

◆ Some keys to successful outsourcing include an understanding of how much it's costing the government to provide the service itself; a cautious approach, which keeps a reasonable number of IT services in the entity's own hands; short-term contracts, which are less risky; and not relying too heavily on any one contractor.

10
Training

As we indicated in the previous chapter, the largest single obstacle confronted by most cities and states in information technology management is a shortage of skilled employees. Outsourcing is one solution, but it can only take a government entity so far. Moreover, the reality of today's IT worker environment is that cities and states aren't going to be able to hire themselves out of this shortage any time soon.

Shortages of IT Specialists

A few quotes from the work place help to illustrate the widespread nature of this IT worker shortage problem:

◆ From Alabama: "We're losing people. We can't retain them. We can't recruit."
◆ From Florida: "We haven't kept up with salaries, positions, or classifications for technology people and we're really shooting ourselves in the foot with that. . . . One of my co-workers left last year; he got a sign-on bonus like he was a second baseman."
◆ From Kentucky: "Right now everyone is experiencing a very bad programmer crunch. The private sector is always drawing people away from you. It's difficult for Kentucky to keep competitive."

Sometimes, shortages of experienced personnel become even more acute—for example, when many government entities suddenly are looking for a large number of the same kind of expert, as was the case with the need for programmers able to fix Y2K problems in the late 1990s. But Y2K was, of course, a once-in-a-millennium issue. A far more common case is found in an individual public sector entity when a new entity-wide piece of software—a new budgeting system, for example—suddenly creates a demand for trained workers that simply can't be met.

Incapable End-Users

Equally troublesome as the absence of well-trained specialists in technology is the fact that the people who actually use the technology (often called end-users) are frequently not up to the task. In research for the GPP, agency heads repeatedly indicated that their staffs were unable to adequately use the new technology that was being installed.

The end-user problems that flow from this shortcoming are found at both ends of the information pipeline. First, there's the question of inputting information properly. A typical problem popped up in Detroit, where the introduction of a new financial management system resulted in a temporary delay in people getting paid because the information wasn't entered properly.

As one Detroit official said: "There are still gaps, and training is a big issue. We had twenty years of people using paper. Now, you cannot process a transaction without having all the proper accounts in place, the funding in place and approval. On the systems, if it's incorrect, you may have to do some research to determine why you don't have the right approval."

At the other end of the pipeline, are the employees who aren't using the data properly, or at all. Based on dozens of interviews for the Government Performance Project, IT systems generally have far more capability than managers—without a technology backgrounds—are capable of using. Most new financial management systems and human resource systems have report writing capabilities that allow managers to customize their own reports—to study information that is very specific to their needs. In city after city, state after state, budget directors admitted that a solid number of managers don't know how to use them.

John J. Zebracki III, director of data processing in Buffalo, elaborated: "Managers still come to me for reports though I think everything is 100 percent accessible to them. All the systems are set up for users to run them. But some are reluctant to use them."

The issue of end-user's lack of training has grown even more pressing as the number of people with access to heavy-duty technology grows. Many cities and states, for example, are rolling out new financial management and human resource systems. As an official in one of these cities explained: "With the old system, there were only a couple of users per department, maybe 200 citywide. Now, there are multiple users within each department." And each of those individual users, who used to have to go someplace else to request a report, can get that information on-line by structuring their own queries.

The notion of putting fact-filled database resources on hundreds of desks has enormous appeal. But as one Denver official said, bluntly, "It doesn't do us any good to buy it, if nobody can use it."

Multiple Benefits from Training

The solution to this litany of woes is, of course, proper training. Information technology without sufficient training is just about as useful as a library without books.

Beyond the obvious—that employees can't take advantage of technology unless they know how to use it—there are many residual benefits to training. For one thing, it helps employee morale. The former CIO of Columbus agreed, "I think it's important, not just to make us more efficient, but to give the people the image that we care."

What's more, training at the front end can save all kinds of remedial help later on. One West coast IT deputy director explained, "One of the reasons we want to offer training is we think it will cut down on the amount of support we have to offer (from the central office). Questions like: 'Where did my document go when I pressed close, and didn't press yes on save?' "

Not Enough Money

Still, despite the benefits, cities and states that provide sufficient training—even for IT specialists—are the exception rather than the rule. The range of resources spent in this area is extreme. In Nashville, almost no technology specialists were receiving training annually when new CIO Richard McKinney arrived on the job in late 1999. "It's woeful at best," he said. "Let me contrast this to the state of Tennessee (where McKinney had worked prior to taking his position in Nashville). At the state there's the Information Services College. They provide ten days a year of training for an information services position. It's been a godsend. And I come here and there's nada. Nothing. Every once in a while, sort of like on an emergency basis, people will be sent to a class. Most things they've learned by buying books and reading them, which is amazing to me."

For end-users, the rarity of sufficient training is even more a problem. As one Philadelphia IT manager said, "I would bet, in any organization, not just the city, that you could not find 10 percent of the people who really know how to use Microsoft Office." A Richmond manager echoed this sentiment, "Training is a vexing problem. Public budgets are always constrained, training money is difficult to budget, while technology continues to change rapidly." In Montana, one observer told the GPP, "There's not enough training for end-users. [Agencies] don't have the budgets and so it doesn't happen. So, everything winds up costing more. You find a high-level environmental scientist, helping Janie in his department because she doesn't know how to run the computer. That's a problem."

The good news is that for both end-users, and technology specialists, the amount of money going to training has been increasing during the past few years. Improved funding is attributable both to a heightened awareness of training's importance and a healthy economy. But, it's still short of the mark in most localities. What's more, if the economy dips into recession, training will likely be one of the first areas hit—regardless of its significance. In San Jose, one source said, "In a budget crunch, training is not considered a budgetary item that is required."

Why Isn't There Sufficient Training?

Given the fact that there's hardly any manager who thinks it's a bad idea to train people (there's really no constituency for incompetence), the question looms large: Why is there still such a shortage of training dollars in most localities?

Believe it or not, some deprive their IT workers of enough training out of fear. It's like a jealous spouse not wanting a mate to lose weight, for fear that he or she will leave for someone better. In Florida, one IT manager told the GPP, "We suffer from the problem a lot of public sector organizations do, that once we have gotten someone trained, they become very attractive to other employers, so it's difficult to keep and retain trained people."

An Arizona source echoed this thought: "Arizona state government lags the industry in employee compensation. Therefore, many agencies have adopted the policy of 'Why train employees? We will only lose them once they are trained to other organizations that offer better compensation.'"

Roy Mogilanski, of New York City's Office of Management and Budget, presented the counterargument, "If we don't provide training, the real quality people are going to leave anyway. They want to use the new tools that are out there. It's worth the risk to train the people. You have to take the risk." He's right.

Another issue, particularly in relatively decentralized cities and states is that the significance of training is not always clear to agency heads. In Memphis, John Hourican, former director of Information Systems said: "We have a classroom, that's right down the hall from my office here. It seats 12 people, plus a PC for the instructor. And we hold classes continually during the year. And everybody in the city knows the schedule. And it goes out; and they look at it, and sign up for classes with the help desk. It's fairly well attended. However, we charge $50 a day per student for training in applications software. Some divisions just say, 'Well we don't want to spend any money on it.' So, we may get one division that sends people on a regular basis and another that says we're not going to send anybody to it."

Libby Mounts, director of information technology in Richmond, said her city provides a great deal of training on-line through desktops. Yet, she's disappointed in how many workers fail to take advantage of the opportunities: "They don't have to come to a classroom. 'Course, they'll tell you they can't train because there's so much going on. They have more excuses than Carter has pills. We've been unable to get all of our departments to have a program for their individuals. And evaluation by the departments (to determine who is properly trained and who isn't) is lacking."

Before his appointment as CIO in 1999, Elliot Schlanger described the situation in his city: "Baltimore had offered a sufficient amount of training, but folks weren't even encouraged, requested, or required to take this training. That's where we fell short."

One common excuse among managers is that their staffs are simply too busy to divert time to get trained. "We're having trouble freeing up staff to be trained," said a high-ranking IT manager in North Carolina. "It's very difficult. I've had to cancel far more classes than I've put on. Not everybody wants it. Everybody says they want it, but no one can make the sacrifice for it. I don't think it's just money. It's availability of bodies."

Then there's the problem confronted in localities that simply aren't in close proximity to training centers. Flying employees out of state for training can get expensive quickly. Large, spread-out states such as Montana are particularly vulnerable to this obstacle. Tony Herbert, administrator of the Information Services Division there, explained: "One of the problems is the time away from home. I've increased our training capacity, 2.5 to 3 times what it was. But when a single individual needs training, they won't find the class available in Montana. It will typically be in San Francisco, or Los Angeles, or Denver."

Fortunately, many of the obstacles to training are not insurmountable. First of all, there is a wide range of methods for offering training—through private providers, community colleges, universities, and training centers, whether in-house or on-line.

That last method—on-line training—is becoming increasingly

popular, and although there are critics of the device, they seem to be outvoted by supporters. Austin uses computer-based training, as does Boston, Detroit, Honolulu, Long Beach, Los Angeles, and Minneapolis.

Keys to Successful Training

Ultimately, the key to successful efforts in training may have less to do with the logistics and more to do with management know-how. The following are a few of the common components that are important to successful training. Each component is followed by some examples of how it functions.

Planning and Goal Setting

Training shouldn't be an ad-hoc kind of an affair. Just as cities and states take much effort to think ahead about their IT acquisitions, it's absolutely worthwhile to plan training strategically:

◆ Division managers in Boston are required to submit a fiscal-year training plan that identifies what training/seminars their staffs are required to attend.
◆ In Indianapolis, individual IT specialists have training programs designed specifically for them.
◆ In Baltimore, the CIO has a goal of achieving forty hours of training for all technology specialists each year.
◆ In Iowa, a training plan is required for each functional group within Information Technology Services. This is supposed to contain a list of classes, seminars, or other education the group or the individuals need. The plan is reviewed at least twice a year.
◆ In Phoenix and Austin, training is customarily considered as an integral part of the procurement of any new technology.

Evaluation

Measuring the actual benefits of training is just good business. In just the same way as cities and states should make sure the technology they're buying is delivering what was promised (see Chapter 11), it simply makes sense to ensure that people who get training are better off than those who don't. Similarly, before training is offered, it's worthwhile figuring out exactly what is most needed and what will be most helpful.

◆ In San Antonio, training programs for end-users consist of classroom instruction on Microsoft Office Suite. Students are tested using a computer-based system that measures the person's knowledge. The end-user is tested after instruction to measure the improvement.
◆ In Delaware efforts are made to assess training needs before offering training classes.
◆ A couple of years ago, Indiana contracted with a vendor to do training needs assessment in IT and other areas. They looked at methods of delivering training, costs, and other central questions.

Carrots and Sticks

Cities and states that are successful in getting employees to sign up for training make sure that employees see the advantage to their own careers.

◆ In Michigan, CIO George Boersma said: "As we move forward with project management; it's going to be the individual applicant who wants to progress in their career who are going to be taking an interest in this. I know for a fact my secretary wants to know how to do this stuff. She wants a good appraisal. As a matter of fact, she has the capacity to get a bonus at the end of the year. If I ask her to do stuff and she can't, she's going to take the initiative. That's what's happened. My secretary says I (need to) know how to do this, I'm going to take tomorrow off, and take this training class."
◆ In Tennessee, according to the state's CIO, "We have each department director sit down with their folks, do a career plotting path, and say what kind of courses do they need."
◆ Several large cities, such as San Antonio and Indianapolis, offer various levels of certification for completing training—an incentive for motivated staff.

◆ In Phoenix, every IT specialist has associated minimum training requirements. These requirements must be met before hiring or promotion. Similarly, employees can't get authorization to use e-mail until they take the associated class.

Centralized Assistance, Even in a Decentralized Environment

As with many IT management issues, training becomes more complex when governments are decentralized. The central government needs to exert influence to overcome many of the obstacles to training discussed above. The city of Seattle has dealt with its decentralized status with a number of sensible steps, including:

◆ An IT training group that meets regularly to share ideas and resources, such as assessment tools and train the trainer programs.
◆ A basic skills training program to bring end-users up to basic levels of competence.
◆ A citywide "desk-side" coach who is available for a minimal cost to provide one-on-one or small group coaching and training on core subjects.
◆ A self-assessment tool on the Web.

Other Innovative Techniques

◆ In San Antonio, when a desktop computer is bought for an individual or a new employee, training is included at no extra cost to the agency.
◆ Austin uses on-line registration for classes—so that anyone can tell immediately whether classes are available.
◆ In Virginia Beach and many other cities and states there is a tuition reimbursement program that has been used by numerous IT staff to pursue college-level classes and training.

In Summary

◆ Cities and states are suffering from an acute shortage of IT specialists and end-users properly trained in technology.
◆ Given the fact that government entities can't match private sector salaries, they can't hire enough people to fill these roles; so training is the best solution.

◆ Not only does training provide competent staff, it improves morale and cuts costs that are incurred by improperly educated staff.

◆ Many cities and states are hesitant to spend enough on training, both for IT specialists and end-users. Even though more training dollars have been spent lately, because of the improved economy, training tends to be one of the first efforts cut during bad economic times.

◆ There are a number of reasons training dollars are insufficient, aside from simple cash-flow problems. Among them: officials are fearful that well-trained employees will be hired away; agency heads don't understand how important training is, and so don't provide employees with the time or incentive to seek it out; and in some states, training necessitates expensive travel to distant locations.

◆ Among the ways to make training more readily available, at a more affordable price are private providers, community colleges, universities, and in-house or on-line training centers.

◆ Some of the major keys to a successful training program include planning and goal setting; evaluating the needs and value of the effort; providing incentives; and providing centralized assistance for agencies.

11

Is It Worth It?

Every once in a while, a news story emerges about some enormously expensive project undertaken by the Pentagon that turns out to be deeply flawed. One of the most famous of these was the discovery back in 1995 that the radar on the billion-dollar B-2 bomber had difficulties distinguishing between a rain cloud and a mountain. This, of course, is not an insignificant distinction to a pilot who thinks he's heading into the nimbus and discovers that the radar is a tad confused.

Of course, such undesired discoveries are only made when new technology is actually tested out and used. And frequently, as with the B-2, they're only disclosed when some kind of an oversight agency—such as when the federal government's General Accounting Office—discovers the problems and makes them public.

The obvious distinction between technology snafus at the Pentagon and those at the city and state level is that a new imaging system for the department of motor vehicles—no matter how seriously flawed—isn't going to cause anyone to crash into a mountain. However, there are strong similarities, as well. The sad truth is that untold millions of dollars are wasted in localities on technology that never delivers its promised benefits. Unless there's a real disaster that draws the attention of oversight agencies, problems often go unrevealed to the public or even the legislature or city council.

Ideally, no Web site, desktop, computer, or network would be put into place without the following two steps:

1. Establishing clear measurable goals for both monetary and non-monetary benefits of the project, while considering its actual costs.
2. Undertaking follow-through after the project is completed, to see whether the promises were delivered on.

In the criteria selected for the GPP, the one that looked at cost-benefit analysis and accountability was the one on which the vast majority of cities and states scored the worst. There are a variety of reasons why this is the case—some of which amount to little more than rationalizations.

Why Isn't IT Held Accountable for Results?

When GPP reporters asked cities and states why they weren't taking more care to ensure they were spending their money wisely, some managers tried to explain their lack of analysis and follow-up as the result of limited resources. But IT experts, and better-managed entities agree that this is short-sighted. If you follow this same line of argument, then you can argue that it's prohibitively expensive for localities to hire accounting firms to verify that their books are in balance, or to pay for building and health code inspectors. Accountability is required in all aspects of government.

Then there are cities and states that argue that because any technology is going to be an improvement over the status quo, there's no reason to spend time and money with rigorous analysis. As an IT official in one Midwestern city maintained, "the need for improvement or the advantages of new technology over existing practices are usually so great that . . . cost-benefit analysis and return on investment reports are not formally documented."

This, too, defies common sense. It may be true that there are benefits to new technology so obvious that they don't require deep thinking to demonstrate. But without this kind of rigor, it's impossible to hold the new technology—and the managers who approved it—accountable for success or failure. It also deprives the city or state of the kind of information that can inform later acquisitions.

Good Management Meets Political Reality

Often a primary reason governments have shied away from holding project managers accountable is that politicians stand in the way. IT officials nationwide complain about their inability to stop elected officials from trying to please their constituencies by spending money on systems, some of which are doomed to disappoint before they're even plugged in. "If somebody's politically powerful, they can probably get an expenditure approved without justifying it financially," said one IT manager in Chicago. "One of the roles we play is to try to stop people from getting things just because it has neat bells and whistles. But if someone is politically connected, there's only a certain amount that we can do to stop that."

As one state's CIO admitted candidly, "The public is demanding more and more technology. And to be blunt, the cost becomes less of a factor. The students at colleges expect to be able to register electronically, rather than through a paper system. The public is demanding Internet access. Whatever the cost, you're going to be in a position where you have to put that in."

The fact is, from a politician's standpoint, that holding new technology investments accountable to previously established goals can be a dangerous exercise—as is most performance measurement. The general public tends to be somewhat impatient with governments who discover they've spent money improperly—even if it's the governments' own self-examinations that make that discovery.

Measuring Benefits Isn't Easy

Even if politicians and managers aren't afraid of the outcomes, measuring technology benefits is a tricky proposition. For example, one of the major benefits often promised by new IT systems is a reduction in the workforce. Such a payback in reduced personnel costs is very appealing for legislators who have to approve new investments. But, in the real world, public sector agencies often don't actually lay off the people who were presumably replaced by the machines. The natural tendency is to keep them on the payroll, by moving them into other jobs. There's nothing wrong with this, per se. It simply makes the evaluation of real benefits difficult.

The fact is, many of the benefits of IT systems do not show themselves in any form of neat dollar and cents equation. The benefits may be found in improved cycle time, happier customers, and motivated employees. For governments that don't have sophisticated performance measurement systems, measuring these benefits can be close to impossible without a dramatic amount of effort.

Some Success Stories in Measuring Potential Benefits

This difficulty in measuring the potential benefits of new technology investments is another reason why it's important for localities to establish performance measurement systems. Consider how the following three cities—which have very active efforts in performance measurement—are able to evaluate the value of IT.

- ◆ **Austin.** Actual benefits of existing systems are compiled through annual customer surveys and a variety of results, efficiency, and output measures that gauge performance of information systems.
- ◆ **San Antonio.** A summary of selected performance measures reflecting the impact of the proposed project on the performance of business/service delivery is used to make benefit estimates. Documentation of the process and data sources is used to calculate baseline performance and progress toward goals. A yearly review of performance measures is taken to indicate how effective the application was to the business process/service delivery.
- ◆ **Phoenix.** Evaluating anticipated benefits of proposed technologies includes use of focus groups, surveys, task forces, best practices research, and expert advisory services. These help evaluate intangible benefits and are used in conjunction with more traditional financial analysis to see whether the benefits gained were worth the dollars spent.

Although these three cities are leaders in measuring the potential benefits of new technology, a number of other cities are taking steps in this discipline by requiring that agencies make a good case that new technology is worth the investment. In New York City, for example, agencies are required to present appropriate justifications for their proposed projects during the annual review process. Financial return and cost-benefit analyses are reviewed against standards and nonmonetary justifications are explained in detail.

In Minneapolis, when an IT project proposal is presented, the expected business outcomes and acceptance criteria must be qualified and quantified. In Maryland, before funding a major IT project, the Department of Budget and Management requires that a project be cost-justified by the state agency. In San Jose, every large project typically requires a benefit-cost analysis and has to be justified to the Finance and Technology Committee. "It's a pretty hard sell," said Jon Walton, deputy director of information technology. "And it goes to the manager's office and the Council."

In Arizona, any expenditure greater than $25,000 must have a justification and approval on it. Another statute requires that anything greater than $100,000 have life-cycle cost analysis. There are more demands for projects costing more than $1 million. Arizona CIO John McDowell explained: "We have a common process that the agencies follow for justification and we train the agencies for the use of that; it's called Project Investment Justification. During our first year, we evaluated $217 million; we approved $190 million worth. And we trimmed about $27 million from the requests. The $27 million wasn't justified. They were trying to apply technology in an area where it wasn't giving them the benefits."

As Michigan's CIO George Boersma said, "It's important when an agency wants to put in new technology, that the budget people know what it's going to deliver. You can't look at technology in a vacuum, it has to be through the budget process."

The Hardest Part—After-the-Fact Accountability

As indicated above, requiring analysis before a purchase is approved is reasonably common. But when it comes to asking whether IT projects lived up to their promises, there's a vast wasteland out there. Here's a sampling of comments:

- From Baltimore: "The city is good at analyzing costs versus benefits when a project is proposed, but not yet good at following up to see that these actually have been achieved."
- From Columbus: "Some of the departments have done cost-benefit analysis. But I have not seen much of any going back to look and see did we measure what we've said."
- From Dallas: "The city doesn't go through that kind of process."
- From Jacksonville: "There is not follow up to see that cost benefits are actually delivered."
- From New Hampshire: "We don't go back and look for performance results. It's an area that we're trying to grapple with."
- From Nebraska: "Looking backwards we don't know whether costs have justified benefits."
- From Delaware: "Where the process falls down is there is no after-glow follow up. We don't validate whether the assumptions that weigh in on either savings or efficiencies are realized. Nor do we devote much time in looking at whether there was scope creep or cost overruns. That's where the system falls down."

Actually, it comes as something of a surprise that so many otherwise well-run IT operations aren't involved in an effort to hold project managers accountable for delivering on the promises made at the outset. Any benefit, based on which money is allocated to a project, should be measurable in some form or fashion, including, of course, employee or customer satisfaction surveys. And assuming that to be the case, there's no reason that the government shouldn't be in the business of actually doing that checking.

Some Leaders in After-the-Fact Accountability

Although many well-run governments do not hold their IT departments accountable for promises made, there are cities and states that do. These following examples of measuring benefits after implementation can be used for others to benchmark their programs on.

- **Honolulu.** The Department of Information Technology (DIT) there reviews all IT requests for return on investment (ROI) and other proposed benefits. DIT recommends project funding and monitors results. Agency technical specialists monitor the implementation of new programs and analyze results to ascertain whether desired goals and objectives have been obtained. So far, so good, but here's the most significant part: for multiyear-phased projects, subsequent year funding is not authorized unless anticipated prior-year goals and benefits have been achieved.

◆ **Minneapolis.** When an IT project proposal is presented, the expected business outcomes and acceptance criteria must be qualified and quantified. During the decision-making process these are measured against the expected cost to determine if the city wants to approve the IT investment. The city follows a six-step methodology with "Go/No Go" decision points. At each of these points, the expected business outcome is reevaluated against expected project cost to determine if the project should proceed.

◆ **North Carolina.** A couple of years ago, this state determined that every agency would have to present a business case before its proposal for a new technology investment could be considered. At the same time, requirements were put into place for departments to use measurement-based performance management programs for technology operations, including developing missions and goals, aligning technological initiatives with business and program objectives, and determining organizational structures and responsibilities. But that's just the beginning. In North Carolina, all major information technology projects submit monthly reports of actual achievements versus plan; at various points in the plan, independent assurance reviews are conducted to verify performance and provide recommendations on risk mitigation. After completion, every project continues to get assessed through its life.

Of course, there's one more important element required here—the guts to pull the plug on a project if it's not delivering the goods. Tennessee, for example, had developed a project with its Department of Education to collect information from in-state school systems.

According to CIO Bradley Dugger, "It was not going in the right direction. It was having real problems in data gathering from the local school systems and interfacing with a lot of the different suppliers of information. And there had not been good definition of the data, with understanding. So, there was a data disconnect. And it needed a little more planning on the business model. We stopped the project."

Dugger went on, "This is a philosophy of the state; the biggest mistake is to chase a bad project down a hole. I never apologize when we say we need to stop this system. We've done it more than once. And you basically build a case, and say we're just wasting the state's money."

One model that seems particularly appealing—especially for those entities that genuinely have the determination to keep their agencies honest in terms of technology investment—is to loan agencies the money for new technology investments, rather than simply paying for them out of tax dollars. Naturally, if there are no promised financial savings from a new investment—but rather improved services—this won't work, and the effort will have to be paid for the old-fashioned way. But if the project promises payback, why not hold the agency genuinely accountable?

Tennessee, Philadelphia, and others are following that path. Tennessee's Dugger explained, "If they can show a business payback over five years through reduced costs, we make loans. They can pay it back over five years."

But what happens if the savings aren't realized? Dugger said: "We had one agency that said they would pay for it out of reduced personnel costs, and then they came back and said, 'We can't do it.' We said, 'No, you are going to have to do it.' This was a fairly large department, and they had to come up with the reduced positions, because that was their position originally."

Similarly, many of Philadelphia's largest projects are funded through loans from its "Productivity Bank." Once again, the loans have to be repaid. One official there explained, "The agency must clearly state and quantify to the extent possible, the cost-benefits of the project and the benefits must outweigh the costs so that the loan can be repaid with interest over a five-year-period. The agency is responsible for tracking these benefits and providing regular status reports to the bank."

In Summary

◆ Though millions of dollars are spent on technology projects that don't deliver on their promises, only the most egregious examples are ever disclosed to the public—or even to elected leaders.

◆ Clear measurable goals for both monetary and nonmonetary benefits should be established and considered in light of the actual cost of the project.

◆ After a project is completed, managers need to conduct follow-through to see whether the promises were delivered on.

◆ One major reason these efforts aren't undertaken is that some elected officials don't really want to be held accountable if this detracts from pleasing constituencies.

◆ At best, measuring benefits of technology is difficult; workforce reductions often turn out not to develop and measuring non-monetary benefits is particularly hard for cities and states that don't have highly developed performance measurement systems in place already.

◆ Austin, San Antonio, and Phoenix have surmounted many of the obstacles to establishing clear goals for IT projects, and a number of other cities are beginning to do so. However, it is rare to find a government effort to make certain that the targets are actually reached.

◆ Honolulu, Minneapolis, and North Carolina are three examples of entities that are moving forward in efforts to measure benefits after implementation. Tennessee, meanwhile, uses a slightly different approach from many; requiring that agencies borrow money from the state for IT efforts—money that must ultimately be paid back.

12

Oh What a Tangled Web

This chapter—about the use of the Internet by localities—is being written in spring of the year 2000. As with the majority of the chapters in this book, most of the information contained here was garnered from hundreds of interviews done in connection with the Government Performance Project over the last couple of years with cities and states. In addition, graduate students examined the actual Web sites for all eighty-five entities studied in the GPP to see how effectively and efficiently they were using this communications medium.

The one unavoidable truth that emerges from all those interviews is that whatever the state of the art is today, it will have changed by the time you're actually reading this chapter.

Rapid Growth in Internet Use by Localities

The use of the Internet by governments is clearly the single-fastest growing, developing area in all of information technology. City and state Web sites themselves are being added and altered continually.

The speed of change is numbing. In 1995, *Financial World* magazine noted "as a dramatic development" that "at least ten states have begun to post legislative or consumer information on the Internet." (The magazine felt obliged to define the Internet as "the giant network of networks.")

Today all the states have some kind of Internet presence, as do all thirty-five of the nation's largest cities. The quality of these Web sites varies, of course. But you'd have to go far to find a government that hasn't acknowledged the value of providing information to its citizens through the Internet. The biggest shift, right now, is to also provide the capacity to engage in transactions with the government—pay taxes, register for fishing licenses, pay parking tickets, file necessary business-related documents, and more.

The citizens are taking note. A recent study by Deloitte Research (a subsidiary of Deloitte Consulting and Deloitte & Touche) projected that the number of people who use the Internet as their primary means of dealing with government will mushroom by 150 percent from 2000 to 2002. In fall of 1998, Andre Pettigrew, then director of General Services in Colorado, remarked that Internet action in his state had "gone from where it didn't exist to where we're getting almost 300,000 hits a month." In New York City, IT sources report that the number of "page views" over the Web increased 289 percent from 1998 to 1999.

Montana's CIO, Tony Herbert added: "We're talking about orbiting the earth in comparison to what we did four years ago. It's phenomenal."

Creative Applications Are Being Added Continually

Examples of the creative use of the Internet for providing information abound. Here are a few:

◆ In Indianapolis in November 1999, more than 60,000 registered voters logged on to IndyGov.org to find the correct polling place, download absentee ballots, and look at election results that were updated every fifteen minutes. When the city revised its trash pickup schedule, citizens were able to type in their address and find out their new trash pickup day.

◆ In Colorado and many other states and cities, citizens can get access to legislative bills in real time, with updates provided regularly as well as legislative calendars. Many states also provide a tracking mechanism so citizens can follow the progress of any bill.

◆ In Massachusetts, the Department of Revenue publishes pages of helpful hints for tax preparation. Massachusetts also gives citizens access to physician-licensing information, including malpractice and criminal history.

◆ In Jacksonville and many other cities, you can click into the city's library site and get into the card catalogue system. In Virginia Beach, you can find out when any book is due.

◆ In Bloomington, Indiana, and other spots, citizens can tune in to public meetings, using streaming video to watch the city council, or other officials, in action. "If you missed last week's council meeting, you can go get it and fast forward to the issues you want to hear," Michael Chui, Bloomington's chief information officer told *Governing*'s Ellen Perlman.

◆ Some states, such as Florida and Kentucky, are using virtual high schools where students can take courses on-line. (In Kentucky, this is used to supplement the offerings of rural schools with courses that may not be available locally.)

Effective Planning for Web Sites Is a Shortcoming

With such a long laundry list of options available for cities and states working on the Web, there's always the temptation to move forward as rapidly as possible, with little genuine planning. An IT director in one southern state compared the phenomenon to a sign he had once seen at a back road filling station, near a fork in the road. "I know you're lost," the sign indicated, "but don't worry, you're making great time."

One common problem has been that state and municipal Web sites often lack the sense that they were all put together by the same entity. In places where agencies are encouraged to establish their own Web sites, which are simply linked to each other by one entity-wide site, there's a risk that the final result will be confusing to users. That has been a problem in Milwaukee, though the city is addressing it. Gary Langhoff, Milwaukee's former budget and management team leader, explained: "We had 20 little mini Web experts, putting together 20 pages. And it's probably a miracle that they were as consistent as they were, given the divergence in how they were put together."

Robert Metzger, director of technology in Long Beach, also

talked about the move toward greater central control, in late 1999. "We've had our day with individual departmental freedoms. Now, we have to come back and give the city a branding, so we all look like we work for the same place."

Structure Is Key

Obviously, one of the most significant goals in assembling a successful government Web site is making sure that citizens can easily find the information they want. This may sound as easy as pie, given the nonlinear nature of the Internet. But, as it turns out, intuitive approaches for accessing information on-line often run counter to how governments really work. Youth services for example, may be spread over dozens of different agencies—such as in the departments of education, juvenile justice, public safety, and social services, to name an obvious few.

But pity the poor citizen, with computer mouse in hand, who doesn't happen to know which agency maintains the information he or she wants to access. "You have to be an expert, sometimes to find the information you want," said one West coast IT manager.

The underlying problem, of course, is that sites are frequently structured along the lines of a government's standard organizational chart. But citizens shouldn't have to figure out organizational boundaries within their city or state in order to make good use of on-line information. Smart governments provide ways to get information and transact business easily—without forcing citizens to find their way through complex bureaucratic paths.

"We're moving toward virtual government, viewed from the perspective of the citizen, as opposed to from the agency," said Kansas's Don Heiman in a 1998 interview. "You . . . explore Web sites that are positioned by agency, but you may not know that the Register of Vehicles is in the Department of Revenue. The sites need to be more functional." Since that time, Kansas has undergone three rounds of Internet design, which have vastly improved the sites and made them far more useful.

"The theme," added John McDowell of Arizona, "is strategic government. Technology can be an enabler of that."

Phoenix's "At Your Fingertips" site has done just that. It is organized by topic from a citizen's point of view rather than the traditional approach that just provides links to departmental Web sites.
Using the topical approach helps citizens to quickly and easily find
what they're seeking. The city had 1.5 million hits in March 1999
(statistics are gathered monthly).

Search Capabilities

One of the simplest ways to help citizens wend their way through
the morass of detail on-line is technological child's play: a search
capability. This doesn't replace a clearly organized site—which
encourages browsing. But it sure helps someone who simply wants
to know the address of the sanitation department or some other
discrete piece of information. In Minnesota, which has such a
search engine, one official explained, "Anyone coming from the
outside can put in basic search criteria and say 'I need to know
about health care' and be directed to the right resources. We're even
considering having ties to local governments."

Transactional Capacity

Of course, providing clear information to citizens is just the first
step in using the Internet effectively. Like most other roads, the
Information Highway is a two-way street. At its simplest, a growing
number of governments are utilizing their sites to get feedback
from citizens about a variety of issues. In Boston, Virginia Beach,
Minneapolis, and many other cities, citizens may e-mail the mayor
or another city official with a complaint, comment, or a service
delivery request. In San Diego, surveys are conducted on the
mayor's Web page, and there's direct e-mail access to the mayor, city
council members, and city manager. In Honolulu, the city Web site
has a "customer service survey" where citizens can make comments
or suggestions about city government. All complaints or requests
for information from the public that are directly received by the
mayor are logged. All requested information from the public is then
sent electronically to the responsible city department for response

within 24 to 72 hours. NYC Link allows citizens to register New York City complaints—there's even a specific spot to gripe about rude taxi drivers on-line.

But that's just the beginning. The real Holy Grail of the Internet for governments is true transactional capability: the idea that citizens can actually do business with government through the Web. "The direction we really want to move is to making it interactive," said Richard McKinney, director of information services in Nashville.

This was clearly the Web area in which both cities and states were weakest during the period in which reporting was done for the GPP. It also is the area in which the most dynamic change is likely. By mid-2000, about thirty state governments were beginning to provide some on-line-commerce capability, according to *Governing* magazine, but very few had anything approaching a broad array of service.

A few examples of activity in this area:

◆ In Boston, the new Interactive Kiosk project allows residents to pay taxes from their home computer or at the kiosks located in various neighborhoods. In 1999, IT officials there said Boston was the first city to collect excise tax payments over the Web. The city also collects parking ticket payments on its Web site and was moving to include personal property tax payments as well.

◆ NYC Link allows citizens to apply for permits and licenses.

◆ In San Francisco, CityBusiness, launched on October 13, 1999, was the city's first e-commerce application, allowing businesses to renew annual business tax registration with an American Express card or Visa credit card. Businesses can also update account information with the Office of the Treasurer and tax collector. Businesses are allowed to submit changes to mailing address, business location, and location of accounting records. The tax collector has committed to responding to e-mail queries from citizens within one business day.

◆ In Maryland, the State Comptroller's Office reports that electronic state tax filing is now used by 41 percent of taxpayers.

Michael D. Golden, a spokesperson for the Comptroller of the Treasury's office said, "It's been growing about 35 percent every year."

♦ Oregon announced in March 2000 that it would sell state bonds on the Internet for the first time.

Easily Solved Obstacles to On-line Transactions

For many cities and states, laws that didn't anticipate the arrival of the Internet temporarily block the path to increased transactional use. Up until recently, for example, when legislation passed that allows digital signatures, cities in California were inhibited by a law that required "wet" signatures; the old-fashioned kind that required a pen and paper. The capacity to use digital signatures, however, is available in a growing number of cities and states, removing that obstacle. Federal legislation passed in the summer of 2000 also eases the way dramatically for further progress.

At the end of 1999, Philadelphia's efforts toward more on-line transactions were blocked by uncertainties about taking credit cards on-line. The question was simple: Who would pay the credit card fees?

But problems like these are just temporary. It's abundantly clear that transactional capacity for city and state Web sites is the way of the future; and that any locality that doesn't move in that direction is going to find itself at a competitive disadvantage. Consider business owners with a choice of moving to one of two cities. In city X, they can fill out all the necessary paperwork for a new business in a few hours on-line. If they do not fill in a line on an electronic form, or if they provide an inappropriate answer, the on-line program makes them immediately aware of it. In city Y, business owners have to procure a dozen different pieces of paperwork, fill them out in longhand, send them in via U.S. mail, and then hope nothing is missing; because if something is missing, they'll hear back by mail, a couple of weeks later, and then have to start all over again.

There's no conundrum here. City X is going to have more businesses moving in and paying taxes.

More Difficult Obstacles to On-line Transactions

The legal questions that block transactions—and other Web site initiatives—aren't the real issue here. But there are a whole series of open questions that continue to defy easy solutions.

Perhaps the biggest question of all is connected to the fact that prior means of doing business with the government—mail and telephone—were basically available to every citizen. By contrast, in 2000 only about half of Americans had some access to the Internet from their homes. As a growing number of services are available exclusively on-line, this potentially disenfranchises a large portion of the population.

This obstacle is even more serious than it first appears. The money to finance complex transactional Web sites generally is supposed to come from savings in cutting back traditional government operations. For example, if parking tickets can be paid on-line, then a city doesn't need to staff counters where citizens can pay those tickets in person. The cost savings in cutting back on staff positions can then be used to maintain the alternative electronic system. But if the city still needs most of the infrastructure for taking parking fines manually—and it's also spending money to maintain the new alternative—then the new service is potentially a costly one.

What's more, it's vital that localities ensure that non-Internet families don't become disenchanted with a government that treats them like second-class citizens. Tennessee's CIO Bradley Dugger explained, "We don't think being on-line is a cure-all. A lot of times the citizens we do the most for have least access. The people who are on-line, pay taxes and that's about it."

According to an article in the *St Petersburg Times* in March 2000, Florida created a thirty-four-member Internet task force to deal with various challenges, including the issue of how to ensure that senior citizens, minorities, and the poor aren't left out of the Internet age.

Of course, there are no easy solutions to make the Internet available to the uneducated—or those unwilling to be educated in the ways of these blinking, twinkling computers. But at least people who simply can't afford to purchase their own computer and modem can, and are, being served in a variety of ways. Internet access is available in many cities in public libraries and schools. Other governments have set up kiosks in public areas to provide easy access. In San Antonio, for instance, use of the information published on the city's Web site is available on public Internet terminals located in all city library branches, as well as on public kiosks located in area malls and grocery stores.

Phoenix CIO Danny Murphy said, "We take seriously the idea that we have access to all people in the city, regardless of their socioeconomic level. We provide workstations around the city."

Marketing Is Key

Then there's the flip side of the effort to make sure those without computers continue to have full access to city services—trying to make sure that people who have computers do use them to access city Web sites.

One recent article highlighted the headaches experienced by tourism marketers in Pinellas County, Florida. The St. Petersburg/ Clearwater Area Convention and Visitors Bureau spent $200,000 on a Web site that's designed to promote tourism and accept hotel bookings on-line. According to the *St. Petersburg Times,* the site, recently renamed Floridasbeach.com, is overflowing with tourist information. However, through its first 75 days, the site booked just 43 room nights. In February 2000, the site booked slightly more (53 room nights)—but this is still tiny in comparison to the 150,000 people who stay in Pinellas' hotels on average during that month.

Many governments are finding that it's not enough to just have a presence on the Web. This is no field of dreams in which you just have to build it for the people to come. In fact, the new services and information available on the Internet need to be heavily marketed. The Texas Workforce Commission, for example, has used the regular mail, paper brochures, and phone calls to the media to promote its free on-line job-match system—dubbed Hire Texas. This effort included a fax of news releases to 900 news outlets, resulting in 140 news articles. Since the site went live in May 1999, use has increased from 40 applicants a day to 200.

And, of course, no amount of marketing is likely to ever replace a basic human desire that the Internet simply doesn't feed: the need to make real human contact from time to time. North Carolina's CIO Tom Runkle explained: "We just finished a survey; we did twelve focus groups across the state and are looking at what citizens want, and how they want to communicate across the state. Citizens are very interested in participating with government, the Web. But they don't want us to take away the human contact. They want another channel. They want always to be able to go back to a human being."

A bill recently passed in Delaware hints at a backlash. It bans automated voice answering systems from public telephone numbers that put citizens in contact with state agencies. Instead, it requires that real state employees actually answer the phone. "Machines cannot take the place of people," said Rep. Tina Fallon, one of the co-sponsors of the bill.

Who Picks Up the Tab?

All of this leads to one crucial question; how are cities and states going to pay for their Web-based growth? Replacing traditional means of providing services will doubtless provide more savings as time goes on. The state of Georgia has, for example, been able to save money by eliminating some telephone banks that required high staffing expenses. Instead, it has successfully offered the same services over its GeorgiaNet system with fewer employees and at less cost.

It's likely that another significant solution is going to come about through public-private partnerships. The economic model is simplicity itself. States and cities have tons of information, for which people will happily pay. Corporations are in the business of finding products for which to charge people. Put the two together, and you've got a win-win situation. Private companies provide the technology and the personnel for powerhouse Web site services, in exchange for the profits that can be made by providing citizens with adjunct services.

The Access Indiana Information Network, for example, has nearly 70,000 pages of government information from 75 out of 90 state agencies, commissions, and all three branches of government.

It's largely paid for out of a public-private partnership. The state gives its private sector partner access to all its commercially viable data, like driver records. The company manipulates this data in a variety of ways and sells it to any number of potential users: such as insurance companies. There's even money to be made from the citizens themselves. For example, Indiana residents can renew their license plates on-line. The service only costs fifty cents more, hardly more than a postage stamp. But meanwhile, the tiny fee makes the service possible.

Of course, there are any number of additional obstacles—some of them not even currently known—before governments can utilize the Internet to its fullest. Much publicized hacker attacks, such as the one that shut down New Mexico's Web site for a week in March 2000 alarm some. Privacy issues are another major concern; once governments are in the business of selling information for a profit, what's to stop them from going too far with selling citizen information to others?

Answers are forthcoming. Unquestionably there'll be scandals and outrages aplenty as the years pass. But what's absolutely clear is that the Internet genie has left its bottle for good.

In Summary

- All the nation's states and largest cities—studied by the GPP—have some kind of presence on the Internet. Of course, the quality varies, but the speed of improvement is staggering from coast to coast.
- Creative applications for the Internet are being explored in many entities including virtual high schools, easy access to the legislative process, and information about physicians.
- One of the biggest shortcomings in public sector Internet use is lack of effective planning. The simplicity of putting things on a Web site often leads to a pell-mell approach that doesn't optimize effectiveness.
- One key to a successful Web site is breaking from traditional governmental structure and creating an interface that makes more sense to a citizen who does not have a total understanding of the government.

- Search capabilities are also essential elements in successful Web sites for stakeholders including citizens.
- As more information is available on-line, the most significant goal for cities and states is to allow transactions to take place on-line, including paying taxes, registering and paying for licenses, and filling out business forms.
- In some government entities, there are legal barriers to easy transactional use of the Internet. But these barriers can be solved relatively easily.
- More difficult to overcome are issues inherent in increased use of the Internet for transactions. For example, how will the transactions be paid for? Will citizens without easy Internet access be left behind?
- Marketing is key. Providing information, or a service, on-line isn't enough unless the potential users are aware that it's available.

13

Case in Point: Washington State's Electronic Filing System

One warm evening in June 1997, IT project manager Dave Kirk left his office after a long, hard day working on Washington's planned electronic filing and tax payment system. He was confident that the idea was a good one: giving businesses a way to file and pay taxes on-line. But he was dealing with an unproven technology, a shortage of technology experts, and a lack of in-house expertise. Kirk was one of three project managers for ELF, the pixie-like nickname for the electronic filing effort. As he walked into the parking lot, still fretting over potential problems, Kirk ran into Steve Kolodney, the state's CIO. Kolodney must have sensed his staffer's concern.

"You know, you really don't have any risk in this thing," the CIO told Kirk that night. "If your team makes it, you're all going to be heroes. And if it doesn't, you're all going to receive accolades for trying." Fortunately, the downside of Kolodney's prediction was never tested.

Six months later, ELF was introduced to the world at a press conference. It was described by Department of Revenue director Fred Kiga as "so leading edge that even private-sector companies are asking for information on what we're doing."

What Is ELF?

ELF made Washington the first state to give businesses a way to both file and pay excise taxes on-line. Currently, 3,000 businesses use the service, but the plan is for this number to grow to 80,000 in the next few years. The Internet-based filing method reduces errors and reduces the time spent by taxpayers in preparing forms. As more businesses use the service, it will significantly ease the Department of Revenue's paper load. Other states have come to Washington for advice, including IT-heavyweight Virginia, which is now implementing its system. Members of the ELF team are in big demand on the speaking circuit.

Encouraging Risk Taking

Three years later, that chance meeting with his CIO still sticks in Kirk's mind. "I've never forgotten that," he said. "You have to encourage people to take risks. You have to push outside the box. That typifies the executive sponsorship we enjoyed."

Fred Kiga, director of the Department of Revenue, agreed. "There was a lot of risk at the outset. You had to provide leadership and encouragement and assurance that as long as calculated risks were taken, there would be no retribution if there were failure. You have to create an environment where people feel comfortable being innovative."

Strategic Planning

The project that would be christened ELF was conceived in the early 1990s by the state's Department of Revenue. "This was one of the high priorities of our strategic business plan," said Ralph Osgood, assistant director of Taxpayer Account Administration. "We wanted to develop alternative filing methods. It was nebulous in concept at the time. We didn't know what we meant, but we knew we had to do something more electronically efficient than what we were doing with all of that paper."

The gestation period for the project was long, and the first concrete steps toward the birth of ELF weren't really taken until 1997, when new Governor Gary Locke came into office.

Governor Locke is known throughout the country as one of the few "management governors" who truly deserves that title. His message was clear—make government more efficient—and his timing was propitious as the Internet was on the cusp of turning a whole variety of dreams into realities. Washington managers took the first steps toward the new project.

As with most successful technology projects, the building of a business case was crucial, said Kirk. All too many technology projects are brought into the world with too little input from the ultimate users. And, in fact, one-on-one conversations and focus groups with a variety of businesses at first delivered a "ho hum" reaction to the idea.

But the project team persisted. They wanted to know what features would be of genuine value to businesspeople if an electronic filing system were set up. The answers were pretty clear: businesspeople wanted to save time and money and not have to spend much time reading instruction manuals to do it.

Concerns were also elicited: potential users of ELF worried about security issues, and the safety of making direct payments to the state. What about privacy, they asked. Would their bank accounts be vulnerable to withdrawals they didn't authorize? The specter of an electronic blip suddenly withdrawing the money needed for payroll the next day cast a rather ominous shadow for many businesses.

The ELF team took their desires and concerns seriously. The next step was to build a simple prototype, an example of what the product might look like to users. When the focus groups were exposed to the prototype, they began to get excited. "You can't always envision new concepts if all you do is talk about them," said Kirk. "When we showed how the features would work, they were amazed. They said 'Wow, government is listening.'"

A Solid Base for Action

Armed with this newly enthusiastic response from the business community, the Department of Revenue in collaboration with the

Department of Information Services (DIS) set about developing the software that could handle the task. This wasn't going to be an easy road. But Washington's organizational structure and rules (described below) provided a particularly good base for taking the action.

1. A Strong CIO

In Washington, the CIO reports directly to the governor and sits on the cabinet. This means, said Kirk, that "Steve Kolodney is able to advance technology issues" at a high level and in the context of business planning and decision making for the state. The presence on the cabinet was of real importance. "Otherwise technology issues are pushed down to a low level of the enterprise and you don't get the visibility or priority and you can't drive forward with the initiatives that you need to," said Kirk.

Visibility is something that the ELF project had in abundance. The governor himself became very interested, because it represented the kind of transformation of government services that he had asked for when he took office.

2. A Partnership Between Central IT and Agencies

Washington is a state that has found the much sought-after "happy medium" between a decentralized and centralized structure. Agencies, especially large ones such as the Department of Revenue, have their own information technology staffs and are allowed a certain amount of freedom to innovate. But there is also a strong central office, which tries to leverage any agency activities to provide statewide benefits. "This was a true partnership and a very effective working relationship," said Kiga. "The partnership leveraged each department's respective expertise."

In this case, the problems that needed solving for the Department of Revenue—particularly security issues—would ease the way for a whole variety of projects in other agencies. "We provided the central infrastructure components and Revenue had their own IT structure that led the development," said Kirk, a DIS employee who shared project management responsibilities with two individuals from the Department of Revenue—Steven Bilhimer, an information technology assistant manager, and Ralph Osgood, assistant director of Taxpayer Account Administration.

At the beginning of the project, the partners put down in writing what their goals were. "This was a very deliberate process to reduce to writing the business reasons to invest in the project," explained Kirk. "Revenue wanted to make electronic tax filing a reality. The Department of Information Services wanted to learn and develop infrastructure that the whole state could use. We had complementary business goals that we reduced to writing."

"And we had the same common goal, which is to provide the business community with a more efficient way to pay taxes," added Osgood.

3. Financial Flexibility

When Fred Kiga and his team decided that they should pursue this project, they did not have to get approval from the legislature or budget office. There was enough flexibility in the Department of Revenue budget so that they could shift resources, freeing up staff time, and shifting about $50,000 of agency funds to hire a consultant. "We started this project with no new dollars for the agency," said Osgood. "We had the study completed and implemented with no additional dollars. We did it by redirecting resources and priorities." (The Government Performance Project found that Washington was one of the states that offered its agencies most flexibility with their own funds. It appropriates on a program or subprogram basis, and does not lock them in by line item or object of expenditure.)

Managing the Project

Of course, these factors eased the way for this (and other projects). But they hardly insured its success any more than the design experts at Ford could have predicted the Edsel disaster or the marketing gurus at Coca-Cola could have known that nobody really wanted a New Coke.

If ELF were ever to become a practical reality, good project management would be key. The development and implementation of the system was broken down into a number of small steps, a "phased in approach," as Department of Revenue director Kiga described it. This reduced upfront investment and kept expectations sharply directed at achievable intermittent goals.

It also gave the department a "wading in" option. It's a lot safer to enter the ocean one step at a time; you can always turn back and head for shore if the currents are too strong. Jumping into the middle of the Atlantic, by contrast, leaves few viable options other than "sink or swim." "There were checking points all along the way where we could turn back," said Kirk. Ralph Osgood added, "With the phased approach, we had a lot of checking points. 'Go/No Go' decision points."

But wouldn't project managers and staffers be risking their careers if they reached a milestone and decided the right answer was "No!" Everyone in Washington knew the answer to that one; it was precisely in line with the reassuring words Kolodney had for Kirk in the parking lot. "If the answer was no, that was still success. We laid out those ground rules in advance," said Kirk.

Following the so-called "proof of concept stage," in which the state got buy-in from the business community, and development of prototype software, ten businesses were selected to try on-line filing and payment for their November 1997 returns. "It was a controlled situation and a controlled group of people," said Steven Bilhimer, information technology assistant manager within the Department of Revenue.

The Significance of Marketing

Washington understood that the "field of dreams" fantasy, described in Chapter 12, wouldn't hold up. Just because they built something, it didn't mean the customers would come to it in droves. Marketing was necessary, too.

A press conference in December 1997 brought the concepts of ELF to the public for the first time, with Governor Gary Locke heralding the technological advance himself at the headquarters of Sunset Air, a heating and cooling systems repair company that was one of the original ten test users. From that point on, the marketing of the new systems always emphasized that it was a partnership between businesses and government. "The ability to file and pay taxes via the Internet is a national first, and it's not just the technology that's innovative," said Governor Locke at the press conference. "This project was developed not by our state government alone but by a partnership of government and our customers."

Newspaper accounts invariably quoted those customers, whose comments were played up in Department of Revenue press releases. For example, Sunset Air president Pete Fluetsch was quoted as saying, "I like it because it helps me get my taxes right the first time. It also makes a lot of sense for business and state government to work together to reduce unnecessary paperwork and avoid time-consuming errors."

Lisa Gifford, president of another test company, Alliance Enterprises, said, "It's great to see state agencies be this responsive to the needs of the business community."

Testing

After DIS knew that they had a good product, they had to make sure it would actually work—and not just for ten hand-picked businesses, but for everyone. The software was fully developed, massaged, hammered tested, and retested. At one point, there were signs that the original ELF software had the potential to mangle other elements in a user's Windows 95 program. This is the kind of threat that frightens computer users from installing any new software they think might conflict with their old stuff; a kind of technophobia that afflicts many computer users at some point in their maturation.

Later, state workers discovered other difficulties: firewalls in place at a hospital to protect software from hackers, created kinks in the running of the ELF program. The ELF crew also found it particularly challenging to be offering a service over the Internet. Bilhimer said: "Because of the nature of the World Wide Web, when you do have a problem, it's difficult to establish a course of action because of the many variables."

Although Bilhimer lost a lot of sleep as each glitch was discovered, because the software had not been significantly deployed yet, the consequences were never severe. "Small failures were good for us. They were learning experiences," said Kiga. This is the kind of thing that people often say after they've finished a project. But Kiga genuinely sounds like he believes it.

Rolling Out the System

By August 1998, the project was ready for the next big step. The state selected nearly 200 businesses to try out the new version of ELF. Meanwhile, the Department of Revenue had been gearing into action to prepare for the new onslaught of electronic returns. They were, after all, the folks who would own this new system; and face criticism if problems cropped up. The project meanwhile won the Governor's Quality Award and some 100 staffers trekked over to the governor's mansion for an awards ceremony. Throughout the development process, multiperson teams had been assembled in such areas as infrastructure, design, testing, and marketing. Now they all had a chance to take a bow.

More Marketing

As time progressed toward a major rollout of the system, marketing became ever more vital. Another press conference in September 1998 announced that ELF was now ready for widespread use. Symbolically, Governor Locke in Seattle (and two other high-level officials at press conferences in other parts of Washington) tore an oversized tax return in half to dramatize the move away from paper. Once again, the press conference was hosted by a user business— this time Mer Equipment, a Seattle company that builds diesel electric generators.

Marketing was important internally as well as externally. From the early stages of the project, the team made sure that everyone in the Department of Revenue knew about the effort. Vikki Riffe, the assistant director for Taxpayer Services, who headed the marketing effort, described the work: "We created an internal and external marketing committee. We tended to over-communicate so that all the employees would be aware of the updates that ELF was going through. We e-mailed general workers constantly."

To help promote the product and increase internal knowledge about it, a general call went out to employees to participate. Managers set up a Speaker's Bureau—offering the revenue auditing staff, revenue agents, and taxpayer information specialists a chance to go through training and become speakers. An "ELF Academy" was set up to give a day-long session to volunteers, training them to make presentations about the product. They then became eligible to visit Chambers of Commerce and business associations across the state. This was particularly attractive to workers whose regular contact with taxpayers often tended to be negative. "This gave staff an opportunity to engage in a positive dialogue—government truly helping business in a partnership," said Osgood.

Ongoing Hurdles

The effort to get people to actually use the product continues. After such a successful kick-off, the crew in Washington has been startled at the resistance that still exists to changing business processes. "Taxpayers said this was the greatest thing since sliced bread," said Kiga. "However, overall there was a reluctance to dealing with electronic commerce. We're slowly overcoming that hurdle."

Part of the problem initially was that filing and paying electronically required a certain amount of effort—businesses had to go to their own banks to arrange for direct fund transfers. They had to make sure they had the proper supplementary software on their computers. They had to install the software for ELF. These weren't major hassles, but the additional steps added to a certain amount of business inertia, especially when it was easy to keep filing the old way.

Often, explained Steven Bilhimer, the president of a business would think it was great and be sold on the idea, but the bookkeeper was not interested in changing the way he or she did things. As any student of bureaucracies understands, a resolute bookkeeper can often have significantly more power than an intrigued president, who is occupied with a thousand other things. "The reluctance to try something new is a dynamic that state agencies can easily underestimate," he said.

Like ducks in a shooting gallery, each time an obstacle has been identified, the ELF team has tried to shoot it down. For example the Department of Revenue is currently in the process of adding credit card payments as an option and businesses can now arrange for fund transfers from their banks directly through the ELF Web site without having to physically go to the banks themselves. Another planned improvement is to make it possible for businesses to download information into ELF rather than re-key it. "It's all a matter of tweaking," said Kiga. "Making the business case and making it more taxpayer friendly."

The marketing group continues to talk with customers to see what changes they would like to see in the future.

Cost Benefits

There has not yet been a formal cost-benefit evaluation of ELF; but it may also be premature for one, at least on the monetary side. The first official funding came from the legislature in the 1999–2001 biennium to the tune of $1.2 million. Because only a relatively small percentage of taxpayers are using ELF to date, it has not resulted in any financial efficiencies. If anything, the state has spent more money than it has saved, thus far. "Right now we're running two business approaches, a duplication of processes," said Ralph Osgood. However, there are clear financial savings in the future, when ELF will have more users.

What's more, there are already plenty of nonfinancial benefits. ELF provides much more accurate filings—there is a 4 percent error rate compared with a 13 percent error rate on paper. Anecdotally, it also appears to substantially cut down on the time businesses need to take on the task. One local executive estimated that his tax filing took twenty minutes using ELF compared with two and a half hours otherwise.

There's also a psychic benefit. "Our people came away with a feeling of empowerment," said Kiga. "As a result of this project there was a major transformation of attitudes. They realized that they had accomplished what skeptics said they could not."

In Summary

◆ The state of Washington determined that it wanted to establish an electronic filing (ELF) system for business taxpayers. Among the most important elements leading to its success was assurance from the top that managers could take risks in developing the system, without risking their own jobs.

◆ From the outset, work on ELF was carefully planned; and a detailed business case was developed before any work was begun.

◆ Stakeholders—particularly businesses that might use ELF— were involved in the process, and their comments were solicited.

◆ Three elements in Washington that contributed to ELF's success were a strong CIO, a partnership between the central IT office and the agencies, and financial flexibility.

◆ One of the most important lessons learned was that new, improved on-line services will not be successful if they are not effectively marketed to potential users.

◆ Even with marketing, potential users are still often reluctant to change to a new system, when they've grown accustomed to using another one.

◆ Testing was also crucial; any major snags in a new system will potentially scare away new users indefinitely.

14

Case in Point: Philadelphia's Geographic Information System

One of the least pleasant tasks performed by workers for Philadelphia's Water Department is heading out in trucks to turn off the water for residents who haven't paid their bills. It's not a particularly fun job—and until very recently it wasn't a particularly efficient one either. That was because the trucks were routed to stop at streets as they appeared on an alphabetically ordered list. So, for example, the same day a truck was sent to do work on South Street in the central city area, it might also be deployed to Southampton Street in the far northeast part of town.

This arrangement obviously didn't make sense, but with 47,000 blocks within city limits, there didn't seem to be a viable choice. The streets were listed alphabetically in Philadelphia's database and that was that. As one Philadelphia manager said, "To have someone have knowledge of where all the streets and street addresses were, would have been more or less impossible."

Geographic Information System (GIS)

This problem described above persisted until the city invested in a Geographic Information System (GIS). A GIS allows cities to handle data in a geographic framework, often in overlapping layers so that managers can see how assets or services relate to each other. In recent years, Philadelphia, like many cities, has been adding scores of useful applications to its enterprise-wide GIS. In the mid-1990s, the Water Department realized that GIS was an immeasurably useful technology that would allow it to manage its assets better, pull together data about assets and customers, and make better decisions. With water lines, customers, and meters spread out all over the city, a geographic approach made complete sense.

Once the department had its GIS operating, creating more efficient routes for Water Department drivers was simple. The geographic database, as opposed to an alphabetical one, now allows workers to plan on-site visits based on proximity of addresses not alphabet. Using GIS, the department began to plan its shutoffs in clusters—targeting accounts with the highest amounts owed and then targeting another twenty-five in the same location.

The results went far beyond saving gas and wear and tear on city trucks. With greater efficiency, collections under the new system rose 67 percent in the first year. "We see GIS as being very important in allowing us to reduce our costs for delivering services, but at the same time improving the services that we deliver," said Susan Lior, deputy water commissioner.

In fact, GIS may stand to transform the way governments do business as much or more than any other new technology.

A few more striking examples from Philadelphia:

◆ The police department's CompStat system uses GIS-generated maps to show where crime is occurring. These maps help dispatchers, aid in the analysis of crime, and ensure the optimal use of personnel. Tracking and mapping crime geographically has enabled Philadelphia (and many other police departments) to distribute their resources more sensibly in terms of putting officers or patrols into certain areas depending on needs. One specific use within the police department has occurred with stolen cars. The police map the location from which cars are stolen and the spots where they're recovered. This provides a means of "identifying clusters of recovered vehicles that may suggest a chop shop or other spatial pattern of data," stated one city report. From this data, the city has been able to identify certain potential routes that car thieves use and started to stop tow trucks along the routes that were towing hot cars.

◆ The Street Department uses GIS maps to record accident locations, which has helped managers make decisions about the placement of signs.

◆ The Health Department is beginning to use GIS to target the areas of the city at high risk for certain diseases. These disease maps help managers to see if there are "hot spots"—areas in which certain illnesses are concentrated. "This is pretty much in a beginning state, but the potential for identifying disease breakouts in terms of epidemiological data would allow researchers to backtrack to a cause if you look at it over time. You might be able to track the movement or progress of a disease," said Bill Miller, administrative engineer for Air Management Services.

◆ Air Management Services recently used GIS to study its issuance of permits to sources operating equipment that emits air pollution. Addresses that had received permits were distributed on a map to see if they correlated with lower-income areas. This has long been a concern of the Environmental Protection Agency and others who worry about environmental justice. As it turned out, no correlation was found.

◆ GIS is used to improve routing and scheduling for a variety of city services, such as trash collection. This is one reason cited for a decrease in sanitation costs.

◆ Managers used GIS to plan for the Republican Convention in August 2000—mapping out, for instance, the route for buses that handle the media and figuring out traffic patterns.

Difficulties in Standardizing and Sharing Data

Most large cities have stepped enthusiastically into this world, but not without difficulty. As the technology has developed over the last decade, cities have learned the hard way the importance of sharing and standardizing data to make the most of the systems. Many decentralized governments let departments enter into this field on their own—with the result that GIS developed in an uncoordinated manner. Maps were internally useful, but could not be meshed with other departmental efforts.

Philadelphia is one of the cities that coordinated its GIS the most successfully. Managers there believe that their city now has the largest integrated municipal GIS in the United States, with more than 100 maps that can be used together—tax records can be matched against vacant properties for example. Street and utility repairs also can be coordinated so that a street isn't repaved right before the utility wants to rip it up.

Beyond its scheduling, routing, and organizational capabilities, GIS provides a way of communicating that lays out data in a visual manner. "A picture is worth 1,000 words," said Miller. "People who deal with a lot of technical data, may have information, but the important thing is to be able to communicate it to the public and elected officials. Being able to see—to visualize through GIS is an important tool in terms of communicating information to the policy makers."

The uses of GIS were clearly envisioned as far back as the 1980s, when Philadelphia made its first unsuccessful ventures into the new technology. At the time, according to Liza Casey, director of Philadelphia's Enterprise GIS, the city saw clearly the possibilities of the technology. But the plans were too broad and too ambitious. "It was trying to be too many things to too many diverse interests and collapsed under its own weight."

The current system had its genesis in 1993, when the Philadelphia City Planning Commission took the lead and started to build its own geographical databases, to be used for planning and development. This included the all-important "Centerline file," a road map that accurately represents the distance of each city street between each intersection. "The Commission realized that they needed to take the leap themselves and that everyone would follow their lead," said Casey.

Support from Major Players

With the clear interest and support of Mayor Ed Rendell, and the head of the Planning Commission, the GIS began to develop incrementally, with the Planning Commission activity becoming the central core for future development citywide.

Immediately, a GIS task force was set up, made up of department commissioners and deputy commissioners. This allowed other departments to become aware of what the Planning Commission was doing and set the stage for a centralized coordinated approach. Early on, the task force began setting standards for the development of GIS applications in other departments. The software standard chosen was the Environmental Systems Research Institute suite of products.

Beyond this, the city needed to make sure that all departments entered data in a parallel manner so that maps could be overlaid on each other. Managers made sure that all maps in Philadelphia shared the same model for the earth's curvature and coordinates. This meant that one map could lay over another one accurately. In addition, it was important that departments enter data on their maps in a standardized fashion. So, for example, the city developed a street code list—a five digit index for every street. This numerical code was attached to a variety of ways that the street could be referenced, so that one department's mention of North Broad Street corresponded to another's use of N. Broad St., or another's mention of No. Broad.

With everyone using the same database convention and coordinates, all maps that were created could be tied into each other. "We were centralized and we had standards that were citywide," said Casey. "In some other cities, the planning commission developed GIS and then the Water Department developed their own. We did it in an integrated fashion."

Keys to Success

In addition, to the standardization efforts, Casey cited three important points that she felt led to Philadelphia's success in this field:

1. **A Forum for Consensus.** Early on, the GIS task force helped to inform other departments with what the Planning Commission was doing and created a long-standing vehicle for

sharing information and experience. The task force was made up of department commissioners with Casey serving as staff. Later, a separate group was formed of GIS managers. This, plus a variety of citywide committees, ensured that there was a strong coordinated approach to dealing with problems or issues. As GIS developed, this helped managers make decisions together about such knotty technological issues as how to identify dead ends (which may occur a number of times on an individual street, but generally don't have names) or to develop citywide policy for such issues as the selling or free distribution of data.

2. **Strong Executive Leadership.** The full support of the administration helped ensure adequate funding and attention to GIS development. A CIO position, which was created shortly after Mayor Rendell took office, provided high-level visibility to technology issues and strong central leadership. "The CIO had to sign off on all technology acquisitions and reported directly to the mayor's chief of staff," said Casey. "Because his office had to sign off on all information technology procurements, there was a mechanism for enforcing the standards." Casey's own position, as GIS manager for the city, was also established. This was a rare position in the early 1990s but has become increasingly common as other cities have seen the advantages of having a central coordinator for GIS.

3. **Departmental Freedom.** Although standards and central coordination is in place, the central managers have been careful not to tell the departments what to do. "Departments still have a huge amount of autonomy," said Casey. "They make decisions on what they want themselves. We support them. We help them to integrate with the rest of the city and help them take advantage of what other departments have built."

The Importance of Central Controls

Philadelphia also has some work to do in terms of its management. Deputy water commissioner Susan Lior noted that she'd like Casey's office to take an even stronger central role—particularly with regards to the issue of maintaining data. With GIS increasing in its importance to many departments, and their obvious interdependency, the quality of databases becomes paramount. Some departments do an excellent job of maintaining their data; others are less reliable. "The central agency needs to play a stronger role in committing the city to the long-term maintenance of these data layers," said Lior.

The future of GIS yields all sorts of possibilities. The city is currently building a 1.7 million enterprise-wide GIS server that will allow all 17,000 employees with access to CityNet, to access GIS on their desktops. This will be available before the end of 2000. As time goes on, citizens also will have increasing access to information presented in a geographic framework. For instance, the city has been talking about mapping air quality, so that citizens will be able to see on the Internet, on a real-time basis, the air quality in any section of the city. (The Clean Air Act currently requires that governments provide this information, but without geographic mapping, the data is provided in a tabular form that may not be current and is certainly not easy to use.)

In the next few years, Casey sees an increasing part of the city's infrastructure being managed through the GIS. There will be a maintenance management inventory work order system, so that when a street light goes out, for example, it would automatically inform a control center, which would create a work order and route the worker for the next-day street light maintenance tasks. The drivers themselves would get the message on their automobile computer screens, which would also notify them of alternate routes to take because of traffic congestion.

"Right now there are a number of ways that it has changed people's jobs," said Casey, "but it's not even close to where it will ultimately be."

In Summary

◆ Like many other cities and states, Philadelphia established that it wanted to build a Geographic Information System (GIS), in order to allow managers to easily overlay sets of data on a geo-graphically oriented base.

◆ Having been developed, Philadelphia has discovered a number of uses for GIS including crime control; monitoring accident locations; targeting health care; and routing of city services.

◆ One major obstacle to a successful GIS in Philadelphia and else-where is the need to thoroughly standardize the data being obtained from a variety of sources.

◆ A key to the success of GIS in Philadelphia has been support from the major players from the beginning, coupled with care-fully elicited buy-in from agencies throughout the city.

◆ Other significant contributions to the process were the develop-ment of a forum for consensus; strong executive leadership throughout development; and departmental freedom.

◆ One weakness has been in maintaining the validity of the data contributed—a problem that can be rectified by strong central controls.

15

Case in Point: Phoenix's Financial Management System

If you visited the Calvin Goode Building in Phoenix just before 8 A.M. on any morning between June 1998 and June 1999, you would have seen a crowd of early risers hurrying to the utilitarian ninth-floor conference room. Armed with Styrofoam coffee cups and pull-top soda cans to ease their entry into the day, the forty members of "the transition team" for the city's new financial management system would stroll past the small dead tree in the corner of the room, grab a computer printout—a list of problems encountered by the help desk on the previous day—and take their places in green, purple, and brown swivel chairs for the day's discussion.

A New Financial Management System

When Phoenix implemented its new financial management system in July 1998, it joined a growing number of large cities that had been taking the same path. The attraction of new systems is obvious—they aid in the collecting and reporting of cost performance data and allow governments to trace unit costs and cycle time. Instead of waiting for someone to run reports for them, today's technology allows managers to produce whatever information they desire. The systems themselves are widely accessible and—because they are organizational and informational tools for agencies as well as central offices—they remove the need for the kinds of shadow systems that developed with previous models. Today's managers can often input information directly into the systems and pull it out in whatever form they want.

Although Phoenix was the first major U.S. city to purchase a system from SAP, a German company better known for its private sector work, almost two thirds of the nation's large cities have taken the plunge into advanced new financial systems during the past several years. Spurred by resolving Y2K problems in the late 1990s, and the attraction of systems that offer "on-line, real-time access," governments have been converting themselves at a rapid clip.

The Capacity Gap

Unfortunately, the Government Performance Project discovered that for many cities and states there's a wide chasm between the Olympian ideals of modern technology and the down-to-earth reality of any piece of electronics. Vendors may be able to talk at length about the magical benefits they can provide, but to mangle the cliché, there's many a slip twixt lip and chip.

"The problem is if they don't use it," noted one former controller after explaining how his city's system enabled managers to get on-line information, approve payment of invoices, examine financial transactions on a real-time basis, and run their own reports.

"It takes time for people to get acclimated," said a finance director from a major Midwest city. "They're not willing to give up the paper files they kept before."

When Phoenix began looking at a new financial management system, its managers had heard these stories, and they wanted to avoid their city joining the parade of the electronically disenchanted. "People didn't know how to use new systems, or they didn't do what they were supposed to do, or they were millions of dollars over budget," said Phoenix CIO Danny Murphy.

Involving Managers in Development

To avoid such problems in Phoenix, a Herculean effort went into involving city managers in the development of the new system, ensuring that employees were well trained and that both the finance and information technology departments stayed on top of problems and issues after the system was plugged in.

The effort to involve a wide range of managers in the implementation of the new system began early on—long before the system was actually used. The city's old financial management technology was installed in 1983, and as with most systems of that era, its functions were centralized in the finance department. "With the old system, the thought was that most financial operations took place in Finance. This time we made a huge effort to determine what happened outside of Finance," said Susan Perkins, deputy finance director.

The Phoenix project team that was assembled in late 1996 began early on to analyze business processes in all city departments—looking into how people did their work and what they really needed in terms of technological help. Laura Ross, management services administrator with the Street Transportation Department, was one of many managers consulted. "They asked what we were doing now, what we couldn't do without and how we could change the way we were doing business," said Ross. "They asked what we had to have no matter what and what would be nice, but be a luxury kind of thing."

Understanding Management Needs

Part of this effort meant looking at shadow systems that had developed to supplement the centralized financial management system. What the project team found was that many departments had, to a large extent, given up on the old financial management system long before. Some 1,200 shadow systems existed in Phoenix—small computer programs to deal with work orders and cost accounting and tracking vendors. "We realized that people were working around the financial management system in a lot of cases," said Perkins.

Kevin Kuss, another deputy finance director, added, "The Finance Department found that fundamentally the existing financial system was not meeting people's needs. We wanted to move the responsibility for controlling their destiny out to the departments, so they could research their accounts on-line, enter their payables on-line and give folks the capital improvement functionality and budgeting functionality they need."

In those early days, before SAP had been selected, Perkins and Kuss were both brought in to become full-time members of the project team. Perkins had been in the auditor's office and had a specialty in cost accounting. Kuss had worked in Engineering and Architectural Services with a specialty in capital management.

Retaining Realistic Goals

Once the city decided that it wanted to use SAP, it worked with consultants at Deloitte and Touche to compare departmental dreams with SAP's functionality. The project team, which had about twenty members at the time, began to receive training in the SAP system in their areas of specialty. Shortly afterwards, about February 1997, the city started to form user groups so that members of the project team could share their training with departments. "We started a dialogue back and forth," said Perkins. "Here's what's available in SAP and how it works. We'd test and tell them what we discovered." At the same time, a subset of the project team was configuring the financial management system and its different modules to Phoenix's needs based on what the user groups said.

User groups, formed around various topic areas—such as capital improvements or inventories—concentrated on their own specialties. For example, in their biweekly meetings, the user group that dealt with the cost-accounting modules worked on a new chart of accounts, developing forms, considering training needs, and eventually participating in system testing. There was also an overview group set up that was designed to rationalize the competing needs of the different users—so that one function (purchasing, for example) didn't get something at the expense of another function (such as accounts payable).

Transition Management

In early 1998, part of the project team broke off to form the new transition team. As Murphy described it, this kind of transition management was first used successfully in Phoenix several years earlier when the new Human Resource system was put in. The transition team was made up of strong managers from finance who were assigned to be the primary contacts for the user departments. "They worked with the customers to understand their needs, and so that they could manage customer expectations," said Murphy.

Each transition team member had one or two departments with which to work. Kuss, for example, worked with the Streets and Engineering departments, while Perkins worked with the Information Technology and Audit departments. "Each department assigned one person to be our counterpart within the department. We could talk about their special needs. Whatever their issues were, we worked with them on that issue," said Kuss. "We'd meet on a weekly basis with the finance director and talk about what was going on and at the same time, we'd meet with our transition departments."

One of the keys to the success of this effort, according to Perkins, was finding someone at the right level—not so highly placed within the organization that they didn't have time, nor so low that they didn't have impact. "We tried to get someone with a lot of managerial responsibility," she said.

A Focus on Training

As the "go live" date in July 1998 approached, training—and lots of it—became the focus. The city knew that between 500 and 1,000 Phoenix employees would soon have their hands directly on the computer keyboards that accessed parts of the new system. A consultant was brought in to develop the training and documentation materials. In-house Phoenix staffers directly provided the actual training. In addition, as time went on, a group of so-called "power-users" was put together both from finance and the user departments. These were staffers who showed aptitude for the new technology and could catch on quickly. The idea was that these power-users would be on-site experts who could help those who were slower to catch on.

Early on, the idea of having automated on-line training was abandoned because managers thought this effort required the more intensive presence of a real live teacher. A training room was set up with a computer that could simulate all the financial management screens and tasks. First, the transition team, including the finance director, went through the training themselves to see how it worked. The verdict came back that sessions were too long. Individual classes were reworked from a length of six to eight hours to two to four hours.

Upfront, managers within the user departments went through matrices of training to decide what sections individual employees needed. Employees, who were to work on the system, all had an overview class, but then depending on what an individual had to do, specific modules, or parts of modules were selected. "Even within the individual modules one person would get different training from someone else," said Ross. "Someone who was inputting information would get different training from someone checking or authorizing. A lot of work went into deciding what training people were taught—so that they learned everything they needed but not so much that they'd be confused."

Using the computer that had been set up became known as "playing in the sandbox." Meanwhile, the power-users received extra training so that when departments had problems, there was someone in-house to provide help.

Communicating with Departments

By June, the transition team was working at a feverish pace, with communication to departments increasing dramatically. With this one-on-one approach, small problems were solved and crises averted. For example, Ross in the Streets Department had become concerned that the new system would require much more responsibility and time from her employees who had to input information they had never dealt with before. Addressing her concern, Kuss was able to arrange for the Streets Department to get temporary help to deal with the new responsibilities.

Departments were visited multiple times in the days preceding the "go live" date, to make sure that everything was working. When July 1, 1998, finally arrived, a help desk was set up staffed with five people who had rearranged their vacations and work schedules so that they could be on call to deal with problems that erupted. As it turned out, they mostly felt like the Maytag repairman in TV commercials, sitting around waiting for their phones to ring. The system had been so carefully set up that the initial calls for help were minimal, and by the second week, the size of the help desk was reduced to two people. In addition, an on-line help feature allowed users to get answers to their questions and access some of the materials that had been used during their training sessions.

The early morning meetings, which occurred every day for just about a year, were a key part of the effort that followed the implementation of the Phoenix system. There were obvious problems and issues that came up, but the meetings allowed each one to be dealt with immediately. Eventually, they turned into weekly, then monthly get-togethers. A group of managers who work with the system has replaced the transition team and continues to hold high-level conversations about the system. Meanwhile, the user groups continue to meet together as well on a monthly or every two-month basis to compare notes. The user group on cost accounting for example is considering cost accounting enhancements, training needs, and other matters.

"I think part of the reason it worked so well was that a decision was made early on to involve people from the operating departments," said Ross. Now, she added, "We have more control over our own destiny."

"Sometimes getting it in is the easy part," said Murphy. "It gets intense after it goes live." Murphy knows that implementing any new system requires many meetings, a great deal of training, and significant hand-holding. Even with all the effort that Phoenix put into its new system, he feels that one of the lessons learned is that even more information should have gone out early on in the project. "No matter how much information we gave, it was never enough," he said. "You can't communicate enough or provide enough information about a new system as it's being put in."

In Summary

♦ In July 1998, Phoenix implemented a new financial management system, as a growing number of large cities have also done. Instead of waiting for someone to run reports for them, today's technology allows managers to produce whatever information they desire.

♦ Phoenix leaders understood that simply providing a great deal of new capacity to its managers didn't mean that it would actually be used.

♦ Leaders carefully involved managers in the effort to see what their expectations were, and to prioritize carefully the elements that could and should be included in the new system.

♦ Part of this effort involved thoroughly understanding the system that was already in place: to see where shadow systems were in use to supplement the entity-wide one, for example.

♦ Rather than blindly trust that the new system would be easily implemented, Phoenix set up a transition management team, including managers who would be the primary contacts for user departments.

♦ Throughout the process—and to the present day—there's been a strong focus on training; to ensure that the system's benefits are thoroughly used by all involved. So-called "power-users" were developed, to provide in-house help to others in their departments.

♦ Departments were kept thoroughly involved throughout implementation; any problems that cropped up were uncovered as quickly as possible—in order to fix them before the entire system went live.

♦ The process of communicating with departments continued after implementation. As one Phoenix manager explained, "Sometimes getting it in is the easy part. It gets intense after it goes live."

16
Making the Grade

One of the most controversial issues surrounding the Government Performance Project has been the decision to actually grade the cities and states. A reasonably large contingent of state and city officials would prefer that the GPP restrain from making actual judgments about which governments do the best and worst jobs in managing information technology (and, for that matter, the other four areas covered by the GPP).

Why grade then? Obviously, one reason is that it gets attention for the results—both in and out of government. But another potent motivation is that it gives states and cities the opportunity to quickly find other government entities upon which to benchmark.

This chapter gives a thumbnail description of some of the outstanding points of the six states that received the highest grades in the February 1999 issue of *Governing* magazine, and the four cities that did the same in the February 2000 issue. These ten governments are the only ones that received a B+ or better in this category; the average grade for both cities and states was a C+ in information technology. (For the text and grades that actually appeared in *Governing*'s February 1999 and February 2000 issues, see Appendix B for the cities and Appendix C for the states.)

Obviously, an entire book could be written about IT practices in any one of these governments. So, we are only highlighting the major points here, taking note of some of the practices that were particularly impressive in the cities and states that effectively made the GPP dean's list for information technology. Obviously, you may encounter some of these impressive practices elsewhere in the book, as specific examples of good procurement, strategic planning, etc.

States

Washington

One element in Washington that sets it apart is how IT gets attention at the highest levels of government. Not only does the state have a very powerful CIO position, its Information Services Board is authorized by the legislature and chaired by the governor's chief of staff. "That's a risky thing to do," said the state's CIO, Steve Kolodney, "because project failure is yours."

Such visibility is risky perhaps, but when projects receive attention at this high a level, the likelihood of failure drops. In fact according to its own 1999 calculations, the Washington State record for successful IT projects is 36 percent higher than the national average in both the public and private sector; based on benchmarks provided by the Standish Group.

The involvement of the governor's chief of staff is only one element that contributes to Washington's success, of course. Agencies base procurements on desired solutions to business problems; not specific technologies that may be outdated by the time they are deployed. The state has a formal objective process to evaluate whether an IT project should be initiated. The state uses a "business case justification," which shows how the project recovers costs and adds measurable value or positive cost-benefit to an agency's business functions. There's also powerful oversight over the entire process. "There has to be a realization that oversight is going to occur whether you like it or not," said Kolodney. "So, you have to make the best of this situation in which someone is going to watch what you do."

The state's Information Services Board also doesn't approve any project for more than two years. Big projects are broken up into smaller segments, and the expectation is that any approved project will begin to deliver results within two years. If at the end of any given phase, things don't seem to be working out, then it's far easier to pull the plug and demand results before more cash is allocated.

The Department of Information Services is itself very accountable. It always has to provide a good business case for infrastructure support. If it's providing services that aren't in demand, it shuts them down, just as any well-run business would, or turns them over to the private sector. For example, the department no longer is in the business of desktop computer maintenance. With the increased reliability of desktop computers, the department realized that keeping a full-time maintenance staff wasn't warranted.

Virginia

Similar to Washington, Virginia has a very powerful CIO. In Virginia's case, in fact, his power goes beyond just internal operations, combining operational authority with working in the private sector to create best practices for attracting high-tech businesses to the state.

Here is one example of the power of Virginia's CIO. Back in the late 1990s, the CIO office acquired the authority to actually take over an agency's IT efforts if it felt that the agency's approach to Y2K was not working. In fact, it took over the state's Department of Health efforts in June 1999, thoroughly fixed the computers there, and sent the department a bill for services rendered.

At the same time, the executive and legislative branches work well together with a centralized management initiative that coordinates the state's IT.

Virginia has established a Council on Information Management that is principally responsible for centralized governance: guidance, planning, resources management, and oversight. This isn't so unusual. But typical of Virginia, it has established the following four performance measures that track the council's progress toward fulfilling its primary functions:

- ◆ The percentage increase in the number of agency information activities that are consistent with policies, standards, and guidelines.
- ◆ The percentage of information technology procurements that represent resource sharing initiatives.

◆ The percentage of agency information technology plans that are approved as being positively linked to statewide planning.
◆ The number of resource-sharing opportunities identified in agency plans.

Virginia has also revamped its strategic planning process. In 1999, it replaced traditional annual IT plans required from the agencies with a new version that must include both a description and analysis of the agency's information resources investment portfolio, coupled with information showing how it supports the agency's mission.

"In the past, agencies would have different people developing the IT plan from those who developed the business plan," said one state official. "Now, the effort is to make sure they focus first on core mission, and then look at how technology can help them implement it."

Herb Hill, state planning and evaluation manager, added, "Since 1995, IT planning was incorporated with overall direction on strategic planning. As agencies looked at business activity and developed their goals, they had to come in and meet with the cabinet secretary and finance people and show how they were supporting the overall strategic plan. Now, we're tightening up that linkage even further."

Tennessee

The Volunteer State does a particularly good job in IT training. The state provides between one and two weeks of training for every technical IT person, somewhat more than many other states. Each department director sits down with their IT staffers, plots their career paths, and figures out the kind of courses staffers need to get where they need to go.

Toward this end, the state maintains an Information Services College for its technical specialists. The college earned the state an award for "statewide initiatives, policy planning and management" from the National Association of State Information Resource Executives.

As for end-users, the state's strategic plans have stressed the significance of training for good computer skills. The Office of Information Resources maintains a centralized training division to provide the service to all agencies. This office offers a number of centrally arranged classes in specific skills and makes sure that the classes are well attended.

Unlike most other states, Tennessee keeps track of training data. But the state has not yet actually used the centralized base to ensure that each individual is sufficiently trained. The assumption is that the department directors will use the data for this purpose. "We have not chosen at this point to go out and ensure ourselves that we don't have one horrible department manager," said the state's CIO in 1999.

In the area of IT procurement, Tennessee's efforts are reasonably unusual (though not unique). For major IT projects, state agencies actually borrow the money, based on a business payback over five years through reduced costs. So, agencies actually have to utilize the return on investment that they speculate they're getting, to pay for the technology. Most significant IT systems are funded through the loan system, which helps the state avoid peaks and valleys in its capital funding process.

These state loans aren't friendly little arrangements like you might make with your twelve-year-old son. If an agency learns that it isn't getting the savings from a system it anticipated, the state still holds it accountable to pay back the loan, on time. If that payback requires laying off a few agency staffers, so be it.

Of course, sometimes an agency will request funding for something that isn't going to produce hard dollar returns, and that's recognized as a different equation. If the state decides that the benefits are worth spending on, then the project can be fully or partially funded out of tax dollars.

One new initiative in 1999 was an effort to implement one-stop shopping for citizens who avail themselves of state services. Explained CIO Bradley Dugger, "The infrastructure is going to be common. There will be a common intake. We will develop the systems, so if a person walks in and needs services, food stamps, unemployment and job training, there will be one intake, and we will share that information so the person doesn't need to walk around to six offices."

Michigan

Michigan has made excellent use of much of the new technology available for managing information; and the state has recognized the value of centralizing its systems as much as possible. Budgeting and financial management here is supported by central financial administration and control systems, including accounting, purchasing, budgeting, and other financial management functions. The state also has maintained a centralized human resources system and a centralized management database from which data can be extracted for analysis and reporting.

One good example—among many—of the benefits of such control over statewide data can be found in Michigan's Department of Corrections. The capacity to easily do high-level analysis there supported a money-saving decision to house more low-risk violent offenders in county jails as opposed to overcrowded state prisons.

Michigan leaders emphasize that it carefully examines the state's core processes when it makes its IT plans, ensuring that there is no duplication of systems. Leaders view potential procurements in three categories: something that is unique to an agency and only that agency can use; something that falls in a core process that other agencies can use; something that falls into the infrastructure of the state as a whole.

The state has been moving forward in providing superior training to its employees. As the 1999 GPP was being completed, the state announced the creation of a formal training program in contract management/project management skills. One particular bright spot: bonuses are available for those who get additional training.

Missouri

The Show-Me State stays true to its nickname in that it wants every state agency to show as much data as possible to other agencies. Through sharing of this information, Missouri leaders have demonstrated, they can save much time and money while increasing efficiency dramatically.

The Missouri State Highway Patrol, for example, shares driver records with the Department of Revenue and traffic accident data with local agencies for improved efficiencies in their offices. The Department of Social Services shares its databases with the Departments of Health and Mental Health. The Electronic Courts/2004 Automation project means the Missouri Juvenile Information System will integrate juvenile court case management and make information available to other juvenile and family courts.

The ongoing challenge in Missouri—as in other states—is to break down walls between agencies that have been artificially protected by perceived policy or privacy limitations. The state doesn't want to invade citizen privacy, but it wants as much shared information as possible.

Meanwhile, Missouri has become a leader among states in its procurement efforts. It has developed a "prime vendor" contract, choosing a single vendor and a single point of contact for the purchase of all desktop computers and related hardware and software. In 1999, the prime vendor was required to offer the entire line of IBM, Compaq, Dell, Gateway, Unisys, Hewlitt-Packard, and Apple computers. The vendor must offer the products at 6 percent over the underlying acquisition price—which is confirmed annually in a letter from the vendor's CPA firm. The vendor also must provide related hardware such as modems, scanners, and other computer equipment.

Additionally, customer service was a major consideration in choosing the prime vendor. How the vendor proposed to measure customer satisfaction and performance and how it planned on using this information amounted to 25 percent of criteria that went into the award decision.

The initiative that led to this $70 million contract won first place in the National Association of State Purchasing Officers Awards, first place in the National Association of State Commissioners of Administration awards, and the 1997 NASIRE Award for best statewide administrative initiative.

One other Missouri note: facing competition for IT staff, the state set up the Jefferson City IT Coalition, which brought in industry, universities, and other partners to conduct joint IT training.

This program was enthusiastically received and is providing more IT-trained staffers for all involved.

Utah

This is a state that stays in touch. All executive branch mainframes are consolidated into one data center, which also manages the state's wide-area network telephones. Even the courts and legislative branch operate on the same statewide area network.

In fact, not only does this wide-area network allow e-mail, it also provides group scheduling and shared document collaboration for all state employees. "For example, a person in the governor's office can schedule a meeting with individuals from any number of other departments and can see electronically whether or not their calendars are free for that time and date prior to scheduling the meeting," said the state's CIO. The system extends far beyond the government's boundaries, too. Some 4,000 nonstate government employees are in the system, including city and county agencies and federal agencies.

In 1993, the governor's office developed a Web-based planning and reporting system called "Plan IT." Each agency prepares an annual IT plan that is project focused, designed to include all anticipated costs and project resources that will be needed. By June 15th, agencies submit their IT plans for review and approval. Each project is technically reviewed and approved by the CIO's professional staff. Participants in this review process include a range of individuals: representatives from the state's wide-area network and mainframe computer group, agency IT managers, and the governor's policy analyst. Concepts are then either approved, conditionally approved (pending more information), or turned down.

At the end of this process, since all data is completely automated, "roll up and summary information" is easily produced as needed. IT can be sorted by project or initiative, by agency or whatever database users need.

Overall IT missions and goals of the state are communicated regularly to each department IT manager who attends monthly meetings. Higher-level executives participate in a monthly IT policy and strategic committee meeting.

This inclusive process has helped Utah manage its IT functions with a very cooperative attitude from all parties. The state's CIO, David Moon, described the favorable responses others have to Utah's system: "Visitors to Utah from several other states have expressed amazement about how effectively this actually works in Utah and leave wishing they had a similar situation in their states."

The CIO cited another improvement, "We've had a strategic IT plan in place in the past. What we did this year was develop it at the cabinet level. In the past, it had been developed more at an IT manager level, so there was less participation by executive management. This year, we made it a cabinet-level process, so there were actually cabinet-level members who made it a strategic IT plan. It opened their eyes as to how IT can help accomplish their department goals, and it established support for IT goals."

Utah also takes great pains to make sure it's getting a reasonable bang for the buck in its use of IT dollars. It compares Utah's IT costs and benefits with those of similar governmental organizations, for example. What's more, the qualitative performance of Utah's technology services is monitored with an ongoing series of customer satisfaction surveys conducted by state staff. The surveys cover the full range of IT services, assessing how useful and satisfactory the services are to their users.

Cities

Phoenix

In October 1998, Phoenix city manager Frank Fairbanks received Public Technology Inc's Technology Leadership Award for advancing development and use of technology in the city. Phoenix is frequently visited by other government agencies and private industry to gain insight into the technical environment, specifically Fairbanks' vision of "seamless service" and a "coordinated decentralized approach" to IT.

Phoenix's strategic IT plan, called Architecture Vision, was developed in 1992. It's a rolling twenty-year plan that is annually updated. The strategic plan addresses three major goals: community, services, and fiscal strength.

In the late 1980s, Phoenix began planning for its move away from a decentralized environment, in which departments employed whatever technology served their own needs. At that time, Phoenix had disparate computer applications and e-mail systems, limiting citywide data sharing and communications.

Phoenix now has a "coordinated decentralized" or "federated republic" information technology management structure. Its central IT office has absolute authority for establishing citywide technology standards, policies, and guidelines as well as setting up Phoenix's information technology architecture framework. It makes every effort to work with departments to encourage them to offer their views and to support decisions ultimately reached. Every department and function has a contact assigned to the IT area. The contact evaluates new or revised policies and standards, disseminates information to his or her department, and shares information and experiences with other departments.

But after all is said and done, inside that velvet techno-glove is an old-fashioned cast iron hand. If an agency doesn't fall into line with a standard, the IT office communicates with the budget office. Presto! No money is available for the project.

The focus on standardization has paid off in Phoenix. There are no more discernible stovepipe, or stand-alone, systems in the city. Every department has access to the city's GIS, its human resources and financial management systems, and the Internet.

Phoenix is one of only a handful of cities or states to evaluate the benefits of technology—both monetary and nonmonetary—after implementation. The city uses many of the same techniques developed for determining costs and benefits when deciding whether or not the investment makes sense in the first place. Focus groups, surveys, and postevaluation studies are used, and wherever possible, input from citizens, customers, and end-users is also considered. Additionally, Phoenix uses multiple performance measures in the management of its information systems. Some measures are communicated monthly to the City Managers Office.

Minneapolis

This city has established minimum training requirements to bring each IT employee up to the minimum capability level in skills required by the department and for the individual position. You'd think that this would be commonplace, but it's not. In most other cities, there are minimum requirements for getting a job; but beyond that point, there are no standards to ensure that training is adequate.

In Minneapolis, by contrast, every IT employee receives training or enhanced education each year. For end-users, the city is similarly diligent. Anytime it develops a new application or capability, the city puts the training requirements right into the budget. "If you're building something new, you have to train the workforce to take advantage of this power," said Don Saelens, chief information officer there. "So, it's not taking time out from your job. It's part of your job."

Minneapolis also has a powerful strategic planning process. The city uses a Technology Steering Committee (TSC), composed of city department heads to create its enterprise information management structure. TSC's charter is to ensure that IT investments are aligned with citywide goals. "They understand that each department within the city would like to deploy more technology, faster and better than before," said Saelens. "At the same time, they understand the financial management objectives of the city. Understanding these positions, the TSC has a shared responsibility to create the annual IT plans."

The TSC's strategic information system project planning process makes IT strategic investments decisions on an enterprise basis. This process crosses all departments and is aligned with the city's goals. Each approved development project is reviewed by an internal IT architecture management team to ensure that there is compliance to process, data, technology, and application architecture standards.

Strategic-level information system plans are approved and funded at the enterprise level annually. This supports new development for enterprise and departmental applications as well as enterprise technology infrastructure strategies. Tactical-level operating plans are managed on a department level annually.

Philadelphia

As recently as 1992, Philadelphia's IT could be described in a variety of ways, none of them good. Then, the city installed its first chief information officer, and it's now a model for other cities. Philadelphia now has one of the most inclusive GIS systems around and one of the largest municipal fiber-optic networks any place. The city also won a series of awards for its architecture and its project management.

One of the keys to Philadelphia's success has been its citywide effort to secure master contracts for most commodity items. These contracts, a joint creation of the mayor's Office of Information Services and the procurement and law departments in concert with feedback from agency user groups, are renewed on a rolling basis and have been in place for several years. For what the city calls "vanilla" bids for common commodity items, it goes into the marketplace each quarter to three or four top-notch vendors. Managers ask for a price on the product in mind, and winner takes all. This reduced pricing by about 40 percent. As of 1999, the city was getting fully equipped PCs for about $1,000, pretty good at the time. The city has done an excellent job at eliminating single purchases that must be made off contract. "Off hand," said one IT official, "I can't think of anything we haven't roped into one of these documents."

For larger procurements, Philadelphia has a Productivity Bank, which makes major investments for many of the city's technology projects. If an agency applies for a Productivity Bank loan for an IT project (or any other type of project), the agency must clearly demonstrate how the benefits of a project outweigh its costs, allowing for the loan to be repaid with interest over a five-year-period. The agency is responsible for tracking these benefits and providing regular status reports to the bank.

Additionally, if an agency funds a technology project through its appropriated budget, without going to the bank, the city's Initiative Compliance Committee requires that the agency clearly quantify the costs and benefits before any expenditures are approved.

What's more, Philadelphia has documented, in the city's five-year financial plan, the actual benefits of its existing systems. For these particular initiatives, the Mayor's Office of Management and Productivity maintains regular updates to quantify that the actual benefits have occurred.

Honolulu

Ordinarily, when a state or city's economy sours, they immediately start to cut back on their IT budgets. In fact, the state of Hawaii, which had substantial economic difficulties in the mid- to late 1990s, has cut its central IT office down to the bare bones, based on the dubious logic that it simply doesn't have the money to provide more cash. By wild contrast, the city of Honolulu, which shared these economic problems, has avoided the temptation to try to fill in its budget holes by cutting IT; the city has recognized that, properly spent IT dollars can ultimately cut budgetary needs, instead of adding to them.

In fact, the city's mayor, Jeremy Harris, has stated that it is his goal for Honolulu to be the best-run technological city in the nation. He envisions the island as being an electronic city, where there's a seamless flow of information between departments. And then, as one official reported, "God bless the administration, they stayed out of it. As soon as the people (at the top) start mucking around in the process it's a problem. The IT master plan—the mayor signed off on it, and didn't make any changes at all. So, every director knows that's where we need to go."

The city has established an Intranet that makes available to employees press releases, purchasing price schedules, telephone directory, finance and Department of Information Technology (DIT) policies, revised ordinances, and employment opportunities. The IT Master Plan calls for expansion of the Intranet with technical support assistance, training, electronic versions of all city forms, and frequently asked questions (FAQs).

Meanwhile, the city is doing an exemplar job in IT training (which is particularly impressive in hard times). DIT provides instructor-led classes, self-study tutorials in video, CD-ROM, network-based formats, and how-to documentation for basic computer applications. Special projects implementing new technology systems may also include training as part of the project. Instructor-led classes are provided on a once-a-month basis, with additional sessions added upon demand. Self-study courses are available continuously, and use of the DIT training facility is made available upon request. Help documentation is made accessible both via the city's local area network and Intranet, and upon request. Special training to meet implementation requirements is provided as needed.

Prerequisites are specified for all courses. Depending on the position, new hires may be required to meet certain levels of computer skills. With each computer-related implementation, training is coordinated by the agency to ensure that staff is sufficiently prepared.

In Summary

◆ One of the most controversial issues surrounding the Government Performance Project was the decision to grade the cities and states. The GPP decided to grade for several reasons including getting attention for the grades (which translated into impact in the cities and states) and easing the process of using the write-ups for benchmarking purposes. Following are the highlights from the cities and states that received the highest grades.

◆ Washington stands out for the attention IT gets at the highest levels of government—including the governor. Agencies base procurements on desired solutions to business problems; not specific technologies that may be outdated by the time they are deployed. The state also breaks big projects into smaller segments, so that problems can be dealt with before they become institutionalized.

◆ Virginia has a powerful CIO, who has a greater range of responsibilities than in most states. Virginia has also established a Council on Information Management that must itself meet four major performance goals. Virginia is also steadily working at tightening up its strategic planning process to make sure IT plans fit well with broader business plans.

◆ Tennessee is particularly strong in training, offering between one and two weeks of training for every technical person. The state maintains an Information Services College for its technical specialists. It has also stressed the significance of good training for end-users, and it maintains a centralized training division. Unlike most other states, Tennessee keeps track of training data, though it has not yet actually used the centralized base to make sure that each individual is sufficiently trained. Tennessee's efforts in procurement are also notable. For major IT projects, agencies actually borrow the money, based on a business payback over five years through reduced costs. So, they actually have to utilize the return on investment that they speculate they're getting, to pay for the technology.

◆ Michigan has centralized its IT systems as much as possible. Its centralized human resources system and management database allow data to be easily extracted for analysis and reporting. Michigan leaders carefully examine the state's core processes when they make IT plans—ensuring that there is no duplication of systems. The state has recently created a formal training program in contract management/project management skills.

◆ Missouri emphasizes the benefits of sharing information between agencies. The Missouri State Highway Patrol, for example, shares driver records with the Department of Revenue and traffic accident data with local agencies for improved efficiencies in their offices. It's also a leader in procurement, with a prime vendor contract that provides a single vendor and a single point of contact for all computer hardware and software. Facing competition for IT staff, the state set up the Jefferson City IT Coalition, which brought in industry, universities, and other partners to do joint training. This program was enthusiastically received and is providing more IT trained staffers for all involved.

◆ In Utah, all executive branch mainframes are consolidated into one data center, which also manages the state's wide-area network telephones. Even the courts and legislative branch operate on the same statewide area network. Some 4,000 nonstate government employees are also in the system, including city and county agencies and federal agencies. The state is also a leader in planning, with a thorough linkage between agency IT plans and statewide plans. Cabinet-level officials are brought into the process as well. Overall IT missions and goals of the state are communicated regularly to each department IT manager who attends monthly meetings. Higher-level executives participate in a monthly IT policy and strategic committee meeting.

♦ Phoenix leads in having developed a potent balance between centralized control and decentralization with its "federated republic" information technology management structure. A strong central IT office establishes citywide technology standards, policies, and guidelines as well as setting up Phoenix's information technology architecture framework. Meanwhile, departments are encouraged to participate in the process, and to innovate and improve. As a result, there are no discernible stovepipe systems in the city. Phoenix is also one of only a handful of cities or states to evaluate the benefits of technology—both monetary and nonmonetary—after implementation.

♦ Minneapolis has minimum training requirements to bring each IT employee up to the minimum capability level in skills required by the department and for the individual position. The city works equally hard at making sure end-users are properly trained. The city has a strong strategic planning process that uses a Technology Steering Committee, composed of city department heads to create its enterprise information management structure that is aligned with the city's broader goals.

♦ Philadelphia, which has made dramatic progress in the 1990s, has made good use of citywide master contracts for most commodity items. These contracts are renewed on a rolling basis and have been in place for several years. For larger procurements, Philadelphia has a Productivity Bank, which makes major investments for many of the city's technology projects. If an agency applies for a Productivity Bank loan, the agency must clearly show how the benefits outweigh the costs, allowing for the loan to be repaid with interest over a five-year-period. The agency is responsible for tracking these benefits and providing regular status reports to the bank. The city has documented, in its five-year financial plan, the actual benefits of its existing systems. For these particular initiatives, the mayor's Office of Management and Productivity maintains regular updates to quantify that the actual benefits have occurred.

◆ Honolulu has continued to spend money on IT management even as its economy has suffered. IT has strong support from the mayor's office there; though there is little politicization of the process. The IT master plan, which the mayor signs off on, is a blueprint that's closely followed. The city also focuses on training with a variety of means for making sure all workers are adequately trained.

17
The Crystal Ball

The truth is that anyone who could accurately predict the future of information technology would be richer than Bill Gates. Even Gates has made blunders along the way to becoming one of the world's richest people, after all: Does anybody remember a piece of Microsoft software called "Bob"?

But over the course of several years of work on the GPP, a number of trends have emerged that are clearly going to be in the forefront of future efforts in city and state IT. Some of these trends are emerging problems—for which clear solutions have not yet been provided. Other emerging trends point to solutions. In any case, it will be worthwhile to keep your eye on the following if you are interested in strategizing for the future.

◆ **Government-specific software.** One of the issues that comes up time and time again is the absence of software that has been especially created for the public sector. Repeatedly, governments are forced to customize software for their own needs; and this is rarely the best process in the world. Smart IT managers would far rather buy off-the-shelf software for their government needs from a major manufacturer. That way, they can be sure that upgrades and support will be available into the future. Software manufacturers, such as PeopleSoft, SAP, and IBM, have attempted to create a body of software that's particularly useful to government organizations. But even PeopleSoft, a leader in the field, has had problems with its budgeting system, which aroused the ire of a number of officials in the late 1990s. Users of the system complained that it was really just a modification of what corporations need and was inadequate for the specific needs of government budgeting. It's clear, though, that as the government marketplace grows, software manufacturers will see the opportunities available, and the need to customize will become increasingly infrequent.

◆ **Eased standardization.** Standardization continues to be a difficult issue for many governments, but the need for easy communications, either via an Intranet or the Internet, is forcing a body of standards on many agencies. If agencies want to go on their government's network, they have to conform. What's more, as the market for information technology becomes more mature, battles over standards are becoming increasingly less common. One stark example is how the variety of options in the desktop computer market of just fifteen years ago has been reduced to two: IBM computers/compatibles and Mac computers. And you don't have very many government legislators insisting they get a Mac on their desks.

◆ **An ongoing people shortage.** When the GPP asked governments for the biggest obstacle confronting their IT efforts, the lack of trained IT specialists came up far more frequently than any other response; even more than the appeal for more money. Of course, there are a variety of efforts being made to alleviate the problem. Nebraska is trying to find nontechnology specialists with the right aptitude and convert them; Montana, Minnesota, and others have raised pay levels, and a number of other states and cities have changed their hiring practices to short-circuit complex civil service rules for IT workers. But the fact remains that for the foreseeable future, IT workers are going to be at a premium, and the smartest governments will put every resource possible into recruiting and training.

◆ **The need for more technological expertise.** Outsourcing and training are ways to address this need. Another solution will be a growing number of strategic partnerships with private sector firms. "By delegating significant aspects of their operations to strategic partners, government entities can share both risks and successes," said Scott Shemwel, director of EDS E.Solutions in

Houston. "When each party focuses on its core competencies, projects are more likely to succeed. Ideally these efforts are part of ongoing good working relationships. By 'extending its enterprise' to include strategic alliances, the private sector is establishing a symbiotic level of both dependency and trust with its public partners, thereby better managing its supply chain and ultimately proving value to its constituents."

◆ **A backlash to over-use of technology.** As mentioned earlier, Delaware recently passed a bill that requires that publicly listed phones for state agencies be answered by an actual person, instead of a voice-mail menu. As governments increasingly try to replace people with machines—notably through use of the Internet—it's inevitable that there will be similar outcries for human contact.

◆ **Privacy problems.** States and cities have recognized that they can easily sell the data they're now able to collect. Right now, the pendulum is primarily swinging in the direction of loosening constraints on the use of such data; cutting through antiquated regulations that preclude sharing information from agency to agency. But it's likely that the pendulum will swing back in the other direction, as abuses begin to occur, and citizens grow concerned about the proper use of information about them.

◆ **Increased Internet transactions.** As discussed earlier, the Internet and government services have already proven to be a natural match. The use of the Internet to fulfill citizens' needs and wants is no longer a question of if; it's a question of what can be done and how quickly governments can do it.

◆ **Increased use of Geographic Information Systems (GIS).** Of all the relatively new uses for technology—particularly in municipalities—GIS are near the top of the list in terms of utility in almost every aspect of government from crime fighting to street cleaning. Virtually every one of the thirty-five cities reviewed in the February 2000 issue of *Governing* either had a GIS in place to which it was adding elements or intended to set up such a system now. See Chapter 14, for details about Philadelphia's GIS.

◆ **Human resource systems.** A growing number of states and cities are recognizing the need to set up IT systems for human resource areas beyond simply ensuring that paychecks go out on time. As a result, the capacity to conduct reasonable workforce planning is going to grow measurably over the next several years.

◆ **More strategic planning.** Ask any of the recently minted CIOs what their first major undertaking will likely be, and the vast majority give the same answer: "Create a genuine strategic plan." Strategic planning is a critical skill that will have to be learned in many future IT venues.

◆ **Major computer disasters.** It is guaranteed that a number of computer disasters will occur around the country each year. You don't need to be an astrologer to make this prediction. The reality is that whatever improvements are made in planning, procurement, project management, and so on, computer disasters are inevitable. So, when the next IT disaster hits, you can say you read about it here first.

Appendix A
Interviewed Sources

The following individuals were interviewed for the Government Performance Project's effort to evaluate information technology. Many of them have moved on to other jobs in other cities and states, but the following indicates the entity they represented during the period of time the GPP was engaged in its interview process.

This is far from a complete list for three reasons. First, a deeper understanding of information technology often came from people in other specialties, such as human resources. Their names are generally not listed here. Second, interviews specifically about information technology often featured multiple parties in individual cities or states. Occasionally, all their names were not recorded at the time. Finally, even the best journalistic records can sometimes be incomplete. So, to those individuals who provided help, and are not listed here, the authors apologize.

States

Alabama, Eugene J. Akers
Alaska, Mark Badger
Arizona, John McDowell
Arkansas, Susan Cromwell
California, George Kostyrko
Colorado, Andre Pettigrew
Connecticut, Robert Dixon

Delaware, Jack Nold
Florida, P. J. Ponder
Georgia, Tom Wagner
Hawaii, Barbara Tom
Idaho, Jeff Shinn
Illinois, Bill Vetter
Indiana, Laura Larimer

Iowa, Tom Shepherd
Kansas, Don Heiman
Kentucky, Aldona Valicenti, Steve
    Dooley, Robert Morgan, Doug
    Robinson
Louisiana, Renea Austin-Duffin
Maine, Robert Mayer, Mary Cloutier
Maryland, Alexius Bishop
Massachusetts, David Lewis, Jerry
    Shereda
Michigan, George Boersma
Minnesota, Debra Bean
Mississippi, Claude Johnson, Karen
    Newman, Jane Woosley
Missouri, Mike Benzen
Montana, Tony Herbert
Nebraska, Tom Conroy
Nevada, Marlene Lockard
New Mexico, Jim Hall
New Hampshire, Thomas Towle
New Jersey, Christina Higgins
New York, Gary Davis
North Carolina, Tom Runkle
North Dakota, Jim Heck
Ohio, Paolo DeMaria, Jessie Cannon,
    Nancy Isom, Margaret Theibert
Oklahoma, Rollo Redburn
Oregon, Don Mazziotti
Pennsylvania, Rhett Hintze
Rhode Island, Barbara Weaver
South Carolina, Steve Osborne,
    Ted Lightle, Katie Morgan,
    Dell Kinlaw
South Dakota, Otto Doll
Tennessee, Bradley Dugger
Texas, Carolyn Purcell
Utah, David Moon
Vermont, Patricia Urban
Virginia, Don Upson, Mike Thomas,
    Scott Fairholm, John Mahone,
    Herb Hill
Washington, Steve Kolodney

West Virginia, John McClure, Sam
    Tully
Wisconsin, Bruce Reines
Wyoming, David Bliss

Cities

Anchorage, David Rudisill
Atlanta, Tom Cullen
Austin, John Stephens, Barbara
    Nickle, Dale Van Blokland, Bill
    Underhill, Brenda Bernard
Baltimore, Elliot Schlanger
Boston, W. Todd Sims, Bill Hannon
Buffalo, John J. Zebracki III
Chicago, Christopher O'Brien
Cleveland, Mark Abraham, Martin
    Carmody, Rich Barton, Chester
    Criswell
Columbus, Peter Anderson, Barb
    Johnson, Larry Ayres
Dallas, Dan McFarland
Denver, Stephanie Foote, Cheryl
    Cohen, Ivan Drinks Sr., Sara
    Harmer
Detroit, Carl Bentley
Honolulu, Courtney Harrington
Houston, Coy Basking
Indianapolis, Emily Duncan
Jacksonville, Richard Saig
Kansas City, Richard Razniak
Long Beach, Robert Metzger
Los Angeles, Jim House
Memphis, John Hourican
Milwaukee, Gary Langhoff
Minneapolis, Don Saelens
Nashville, Richard McKinney
New Orleans, Earl Kilbride
New York City, Bill Keller, Allan
    Dobrin, Adam Barsky, Brian
    Cohen, Roy Mogilanski, Tony
    Longo

Philadelphia, Karl Bortnick, Jackie
    Henry, Brian Anderson
Phoenix, Danny Murphy, Don Egin-
    ton, Rob Sweeney, Carl Myers
Richmond, Libby Mounts
San Antonio, Morris Chase, Joyce
    Maguire

San Diego, Richard Wilken
San Francisco, Ed Harrington
San Jose, Jon Walton
Seattle, Dwight Dively, Matthew
    Lampe
Virginia Beach, David Sullivan
Washington, D.C., Suzanne Peck

Appendix B
Cities

The following text ran in the February 2000 issue of *Governing* magazine. The grades listed here were arrived at through a consensus process involving both reporters and editors at *Governing* and academics at the Maxwell School of Citizenship and Public Affairs at Syracuse University. They represent only the grades given in Information Technology—one of the five management areas covered. Understandably, a handful of cities took exception to the text or the evaluation. What's more, given the rapid pace of change in IT, it's unquestionably true that some of the comments and evaluations would be altered were the write-ups being done today. However, for the purpose of this appendix, none of the text has been altered from the original magazine article, as published.

Anchorage: C

Anchorage is the only one of the 35 top revenue-ranking cities that doesn't use master contracts for procuring PCs. The main reason is the city's municipal code, which makes such a step difficult to implement. "If a department wants 10 PCs, it's going to take at least a month if everything goes smoothly," says David Rudisill, the director of management information systems, "or three months if it doesn't."

The city has an enterprise-wide strategic IT plan, but as Rudisill admits, "It is hopelessly obsolete." Departments are supposed to do their own strategic planning, but Rudisill explains that the city "stopped requiring it, so they stopped doing it. It makes our planning very difficult."

On the positive side, Anchorage's technology is well standardized. Investments have been made in new financial management and human resources information systems, parts of which are already in place. This spring, Anchorage will be saying good-bye to its old legacy budgeting system.

Atlanta: D+

A project manager was brought in to prepare the city for Y2K, then left in a storm of controversy in July 1999. Much work was lost. So it was a mad scramble through year's end, and other projects were ignored in the confusion. Now, Atlanta plans to address them.

There are quite a few serious ones to work on. To start with, says Tom Cullen, director of management and information services, "there aren't standards for anything. There are independent contractors working all over the place. . . . It's a miracle that we're not crashing more than we are."

Atlanta's Web site gives almost no financial information, very little about major government agencies, has no current capacity to apply for licenses or permits, and offers few clues about doing business with the city.

On the positive side, the city is reasonably strong in training IT specialists. Procurement policies are somewhat more flexible than in many other cities. And new enterprise-wide systems will help a great deal once they're properly implemented and staff is sufficiently trained.

Austin: B

Austin is committed to a thorough decentralization of its IT management. While there are clear benefits to giving departments a fair amount of control, there are some concerns that the result will be small and costly systems with lots of shiny bells and whistles. Meanwhile, its citywide systems are clearly strong and only getting better.

The city's strategic IT plan is now seven years old, but it was sufficiently far-reaching that it continues to guide many of the city's efforts. A technology committee, formed with managers from large departments, ensures that thought is given to the future, even if a new written plan hasn't emerged.

Austin's Web site doesn't currently support many citizen transactions, but the city is clearing up the security-related obstacles to that kind of use. When the process is finished, people will be able to pay parking tickets on the Internet, and vendors will be able to register to do business with the city.

Baltimore: C

"I know that talk is cheap," says Baltimore's CIO, Elliot Schlanger, "but there's sufficient evidence that this city is taking the proper steps in terms of IT to bootstrap itself into the new millennium. There's a lot of pent-up demand."

Schlanger has only been in office since last April, but he seems to be making progress. There was virtually no IT standardization prior to his arrival; now, the city is developing a solid architecture. The importance of IT training also has been elevated, although it's still hardly a bright spot.

Enterprise-wide systems—installed to handle financial management and human resources—haven't served the city very well so far. But a new financial management system should get better information to managers more quickly than ever before. The current human resources information system is of marginal use for decision-making; a new one is expected to come on line this year.

Baltimore has a strategic plan for information technology, but an anticipated update is six months behind schedule because resources were allocated to Y2K and the new financial program. "No excuses," Schlanger says. "We're late."

Boston: B

Many of Boston's chronic difficulties in personnel management—and in quite a few other areas as well—ultimately stem from the obsolete computer systems that have made it hard to do analysis.

Even the city's payroll has been handled out of three different payroll systems.

But that is changing, and the changes should improve the city's efficiency in agencies all across the chart. There is a brand-new integrated information system that serves both human resources and financial management, and executives are being trained to make use of it. Unfortunately, the budgeting portion of financial management isn't integrated into the new system, but the city plans to add that element to the package in the future.

Boston's Web site isn't much, but the city has made major leaps in bringing the Internet to the public. Residents can pay taxes from their home computer or at kiosks located in various neighborhoods. All 128 of the city's schools are hooked up to an Internet gateway.

Buffalo: C

An early draft of Buffalo's new charter provided that, under the revised administrative structure, the IT director would report to the mayor. But politics intervened, so as of July, he will report to a triumvirate made up of the mayor, the controller, and the council president. It doesn't sound like an ideal way to make decisions.

Some important decisions and changes need to be made. Training for IT specialists has been a real disaster here; this is the first year in six that any training money at all has been made available in the budget. The only preparation managers have received has been on their own time.

With this context, it's a little surprising to discover that much of Buffalo's technology is pretty good. Most of it fits into a neatly integrated architecture. A new data warehouse allows users to extract information easily about financial management and human resources.

Chicago: B-

Chicago has been saddled with sub-par information technology that relies on multiple systems to provide a hodgepodge of data to managers. But this is being replaced by a unitary ERP (for enterprise resource planning) system that should catapult city government into the twenty-first century. Rollout will begin this fall.

Chicago's five-year strategic planning effort is strong. It utilizes input from an IT steering committee that includes representatives from every city department. As a result of the planning process, a city database has been created, allowing departments to share information on property, objects, and companies and to be certain they are referring to the same record.

The city has outsourced the support of network and desktop services to Unisys. This arrangement appears successful so far, and customer satisfaction surveys are planned.

Cleveland: C-

Cleveland has a long way to go in this category. It is the only city among the 35 largest, for example, that has resisted the active use of e-mail. There is little access to the mayor through e-mail, and most employees cannot use it to communicate with the outside world. The city's presence on the Internet is only about six months old, and the Web site is weak, short on both useful information and transactional capability.

On the brighter side, Cleveland has successfully implemented purchasing standards for most of its information technology systems, particularly important in a resource-short city with no extra cash to spend on noncompatible purchases. The government is very thorough in determining the benefits of potential new acquisitions.

A new financial management information system is being installed, and should, as staff is trained to use it, provide a good deal more information to managers. The use of IT in human resources management, however, remains a problem. Small desktop databases for maintaining personnel records are in place but have to be supplemented with paper-based systems.

Columbus: D+

Columbus hired its first chief technology officer in May 1998. Much of his initial effort focused on Y2K. Now, the city must redirect its effort toward addressing a host of problems connected to IT itself.

Columbus has no official strategic information plan in place, although one is coming. Training for IT professionals has been way below par. Because IT staff are scarce, the tendency has been to keep them hard at work, rather than showing them how to work more efficiently.

Meanwhile, the city doesn't benefit from a great deal of information supported by technology. Except for a new financial management system, which is still in its buggy stages, the city lacks integrated systems to help make management decisions. And even though Columbus is looking at bringing in a much-needed personnel information system, the problem of integrating that data with the financial management data appears to be beyond current capacity.

Dallas: D+

IT has long been a mess in Dallas. Most of the information systems in the city aren't integrated, and except for the financial management system (which works pretty well), it's difficult to get access to the data that exists. "If you wanted to know how much sick leave every person in the city has had," says the CIO, Dan McFarland, "we'd have to go to several applications. I was brought here to change that."

There are plenty of other changes that need to be made as well. Standardization of systems is just in its beginning stages. The police, city attorney, fire department, and water department each have their own local-area networks. There are scores of different permutations and combinations of desktop software. "The city has historically been deeply decentralized," McFarland says. "We're going to attempt to turn it around in a dramatic way."

Things do seem to be on the way toward improvement. In the few months since McFarland arrived as the city's first CIO, a long-term strategic plan has been developed and is going through an approval process. There also has been noticeable progress in technology training procedures for city employees.

Denver: C+

Denver is making solid progress in information technology, but it still has far to go. No citywide IT strategic plan currently exists, and a number of pockets of technology aren't integrated or even compatible with others. The city says it is in the process of developing a strategic plan, which should be completed by the end of the summer, and is pursuing standardization aggressively, with sufficient input from the agencies that the process seems to be meeting minimal resistance.

The city's enterprise-wide financial management and human resources information systems have long needed an update, and they are getting one. Basic components are already up and running (they had to be to get the city ready for Y2K). A number of modules still remain to be implemented.

The city's Web site has great budget and strategic planning information, but it could stand improvement in explaining the activities of individual departments. There is an impressive mechanism for job application on-line.

Detroit: B-

Detroit has a sensible information planning process that balances departmental thinking with the need for central governance. The IT department starts by trying to understand the agencies' business requirements, then it figures out how technology can help. From there, a strategic vision for the city's IT is developed.

Of course, even the best-laid plans can go awry. Detroit desperately needed a new financial management information system for years. When city officials got the funding, they moved a little too fast. "We put in a system that typically takes three to five years in two years," says Carl Bentley, the city's CIO.

The good news is that standard financial transactions—such as check-processing and collections—have improved dramatically. The bad news is that replacing an inefficient paper-based system almost overnight with a brand-new high-tech process resulted in glitches. "We had some situations," says Bentley, "where it took longer to pay people, because the information wasn't entered properly."

Meanwhile, plans for an up-to-date human resources information system have been delayed. Detroit simply lacks the resources to implement another big new piece of technology while trying to iron out glitches that the last one created.

Honolulu: B+

Honolulu has poured $18 million into IT projects since 1998—even while the city has been under tight fiscal constraints. The city has a strong CIO, an excellent IT planning process and a carefully enforced set of well-developed standards.

One particularly impressive element in Hawaii's capital is a true paperless permit system, designed to accept applications, track them through the approval process and integrate all the steps necessary for issuance. In some cases, this has cut permit approval time from weeks to days.

Although there are some weaknesses in enterprise-wide systems, Honolulu is addressing many of them. Its old budget information system is being replaced with one that will provide much better decision-making capacity. Perhaps the biggest weakness is in human resources. The city currently has little more than payroll information, and will soon upgrade to a Web-based monitoring system that will allow HR personnel to track an employee from application to retirement.

The city's Web site is generally strong, and allows people to apply for jobs on-line. Honolulu maintains 14 satellite city halls, which are networked so that citizens can complete almost any transaction they want from any of them.

Houston: C-

Houston has a history of decentralized information technology. Police, fire, health, human services, parks, and recreation all go their own way, without much effort at coordination. Consequently, there's a fair amount of redundancy. The issue came to the fore as city officials moved to deal with Y2K, and realized they needed to do something to cut down on the proliferation of separate IT projects scattered about. "It's a real headache," says one.

The picture is brighter in finance. Financial information systems are fully integrated, and the city would like to standardize much of its technology to be compatible with this network. The financial process is run by an Information Systems Advisory Committee, which develops standards, policies and procedures that are then approved by the director of finance and administration.

Houston hasn't filled a long-standing opening for a CIO. The city's leaders have been waiting for outside consultants to develop a technology plan before they hire one.

Indianapolis: B

This is another success story of the Goldsmith years. In the early 1990s, a city report acknowledges, "Indianapolis had few computers, no enterprise standardization, small pieces of the organization doing their own thing, no connectivity between departments and often between computers in the same department, and no connectivity to the outside world."

In the past few years, however, the city has developed a reasonably mature IT architecture. The financial and human resource information systems don't provide the easiest access to information, but they're useful. And the speedy hiring is largely attributable to IT improvement.

Indianapolis has privatized many of its information technology processes by using a contractor that provides data center management and supports local- and wide-area networks, application development and maintenance efforts. Although there have been some hitches (the contractor hasn't been getting the best prices for PCs, for example), by and large the experiment has been successful.

Indianapolis' Web site is excellent. When the trash pickup schedule was revised, citizens were able to type in their addresses and find out their new pickup day. The city is also ahead of the curve at providing transaction-based services. Parking tickets can be paid on-line, and businesses needing improvement permits can use the Internet to purchase them and process the paperwork.

Jacksonville: C

Jacksonville has a solid financial management system, but managers cannot access the data easily from their own desktops. They must go to the comptroller's office to put together reports. The human resources information system isn't strong, either. It requires various manual steps and delays the hiring process. A new system is scheduled for introduction in January 2001.

On the positive side, the city is making dramatic strides toward obtaining real-time information from field-based staffers immediately available for analysis. Police, for example, carry laptops that feed into a central system and produce useful reports about public safety.

There is a chief information officer in Jacksonville, technically called "chief of information technologies," who reports to the director of the Department of Administration and Finance. There is a city Web site, but it is short on financial information and allows users minimal ability to conduct governmental transactions.

Kansas City: C

After much effort, Kansas City has a reasonable number of standards in place for its IT procurements. But there's still much work to be done. For example, the city has two fleet management information systems. Its fire, police, and ambulance dispatch systems don't work together right now, so police have no idea if a fire truck is on its way to the scene.

The city recently brought in a new budgeting information system, which is integrated into the broader financial management system. But human resources information is still weak.

The city's Web site stands out in clarity of presentation. It features a "neighborhood network," which gives users access to much property information, including code violations, ownership data and neighborhood demographics.

Long Beach: B

In general, Long Beach has managed IT operations efficiently. Its enterprise-wide systems are not the easiest to use, but they provide most of the core functions the city needs. There is a sensible emphasis on making sure the equipment purchased fits the requirements.

Most IT investments have to be budgeted out of departments' own funds. Now, the city is stepping in to pick up more of the departments' IT costs. With some more money in its pockets, the city needs to develop more rigorous means for focusing on cost savings or promised service improvements.

Long Beach is an innovator in IT procurement. It allows a modified RFP process, in which negotiation with vendors replaces a rigid, document-based arrangement. This has the potential of saving much time and money.

Los Angeles: C-

Los Angeles doesn't really have an integrated human resources information system, other than for payroll functions. It was in the process of procuring one not long ago, but "the project stalled with technical problems and management problems," according to Jim House, chief administrative analyst. As the year 2000 approached, it became clear that the planned system probably wouldn't support the transaction volume expected in the city. The relationship with the vendor soured when the vendor refused to support the version of the software the city had originally contracted for. The bottom line is that L.A. has spent about $20 million, still has an antiquated HR information system, and hasn't quite decided where to go from here.

The city is generating its first genuine strategic plan for information technology. It's also trying to drive departments toward standardization—and that's good—but it's on a rocky road. Many departments have the power to act independently, ignoring standards. This has made it difficult for the city to move toward an integrated financial management system.

Obtaining new systems can be incredibly time-consuming in L.A., thanks to purchasing restrictions imposed by either the council or mayor. To buy anything, the city must be assured that the vendor pays all its employees sufficiently, has a reasonable child care policy and doesn't do business in a proscribed foreign country, such as Myanmar (Burma). And on and on.

Memphis: C

A year or two from now, information technology in Memphis will look dramatically different from the way it looks today. The mayor has decided to outsource the entire IT effort, including its management. The prime objectives are cost savings and access to a larger pool of properly trained information specialists.

For now, though, IT here is no prize-winner. Creative ideas are tried, but more often than not, they are impeded by bureaucratic constraints. For example, training is available for employees in the use of technology, at a reasonable $50 a day per student, but many of the individual departments have refused to spend any money on it. The purchase of new equipment can be hampered by a purchasing department that sometimes ignores the special needs of IT procurements. Agencies have been told to release information about their activities to the municipal Web site, but the response has been poor, and only minimal information is available on-line.

One strong point: in 1993, Memphis developed a citywide strategic plan that included replacement of an old mainframe computer with a fully integrated client/server financial management system that included some human resource applications. One result was that the city was ready for Y2K long before many others.

Milwaukee: B-

At one time, Milwaukee's IT management was tightly centralized, with a monolithic structure that handed down dictates from on high. Then it shifted to a decentralized system, described by one official as "a 25-headed monster." Now the city has made sensible steps to come to a balance between the two. The difficult job of striking this balance is the assignment of a new Information Technology Management Division.

For the past few years, in the absence of a strong central IT function, the city budget office has more or less filled the job. One positive side effect: departments have been forced to develop strong budgetary justifications for their new projects.

Milwaukee has a new financial management information system and upgrades to its human resources technology. It also has one of the most elaborate mechanisms in the country for manipulating performance information. The system captures outcome and management indicators and links them to broad strategic goals. In the near future, departments with good data going in will be able to use the system to make decisions about how to allocate resources.

Minneapolis: A-

Strategic IT planning is about as good here as anywhere in the country, and consistent standards are in place for almost all information technology.

The human resources information system can be set up to send out notifications automatically whenever a personnel evaluation has been scheduled, send a copy of the performance evaluation to be completed, and then store the results. This is a major breakthrough in the use of IT for human resources. It's a new system, so it's not in general use throughout the city bureaucracy yet. But it has enormous potential.

Minneapolis relies on a data warehouse to capture and accumulate useful information. Although the warehouse doesn't help managers create their own reports, as ideally it should, the city knows that's a weakness and is working on it. At the same time, IT officials are trying to improve the utility of the city's budgeting system.

The Minneapolis Web site is short on transactional utility, "but that's going to be rolling off really fast," promises the city's CIO, Don Saelens.

Nashville: D+

"We've built a huge computer network piece by piece, without much of an idea of what it should look like when finished," says Richard McKinney, Nashville's new director of information technology. "If they had it to do over again, they wouldn't build it the way it is now."

The fact is, although the city has been putting standards into place, Nashville's computer systems aren't very good at sharing information internally or externally. When a department requests money for a particular IT system, it rarely has any form of cost-benefit data to support the request. Training for technology specialists is "woeful at best," McKinney admits. Fortunately, training for end-users is somewhat better.

One forward step has been implementation of a new financial management system. It took the city quite a while to implement it, so it's not the latest technology. But it appears stable and reliable. Nashville is now discussing introduction of a much-needed HR system.

New Orleans: B-

New Orleans IT has come a long way in the last few years. The city has a tight set of standards in place, enforced by a central IT office. Though a few old stovepipe systems are still in place, most technology complies with the standards pretty well. Departments have an on-line connection to a financial information system, and last year the city implemented a personnel and payroll information system that will enable it to do on-line processing of personnel changes, automatically compute retroactive pay and allow direct deposit of pay checks.

With the notable exception of its police component, the citywide Web site is weak. It's cluttered and slow. There is little information about constituent service, budget priorities or how to do business with the city.

New York City: B

Strategic planning for IT in New York is strong. A new technology steering committee has developed standards to ensure that agencies can't get procurement funding without approval. Standardization has come a long way as a result.

The city is replacing 11 systems built over the past 20 years with a single, integrated financial management information system. Its human resources system is below par, but a new one should be in place within 18 months. New York was the first major city to use technology to organize its crime-fighting efforts, contributing to the now-famous drop in its crime rate.

The city's Web site, NYC Link, provides a great deal of information and allows citizens to apply for permits and licenses and even complain about rude cab drivers on-line. New Yorkers can use public kiosks to pay parking tickets or obtain birth certificates. Many of these processes will soon be available through the Internet as well.

One significant fly in the city's IT ointment: collection of property and sales taxes is far less efficient than modern technology permits.

Philadelphia: B+

The forward motion in Philadelphia's IT has been nothing short of miraculous since 1993, when the city installed its first chief information officer. The city now makes information of many kinds available for its managers. Implementation of a data warehouse will improve matters still more by easing access to data where it is currently difficult, especially in the areas of health and welfare. An overhaul of the HR data system is on the drawing boards. An Intranet-based workforce planning information system has been implemented.

The city has a very good strategic information planning process, although not one that is fully immune to political pressure. One IT official complains that political considerations sometimes overrule sensible planning. To help alleviate that, the city's CIO is strongly recommending that Philadelphia create a central steering committee for IT. That could help forge consensus about procurement decisions strong enough to resist outside pressures.

Phoenix: A-

Phoenix uses what it calls a "coordinated decentralized approach" to information management. This seems to work exceptionally well, combining maximum input from agencies with a powerful central control over the general direction the city is heading in. Departmental barriers and turf fights over IT have all but faded away in Phoenix.

Managers use the technology continually to perform their tasks better, in citywide decision making as well as in specific agencies. For example, Phoenix's education and youth information system is an enterprise-wide Intranet system that allows managers to see what youth-based programs are being offered by various departments, where, when and by whom.

The city had problems implementing its new budget information system; the technology that was purchased wasn't powerful enough for a government Phoenix's size. The appropriate changes were made, but the system had to be held out of use for nine months.

Phoenix's Web site is relatively strong, and will soon benefit from the capacity to perform more transactions.

Richmond: C

Richmond produces a strategic information plan (called its "automation plan") that defines the projects it will be embarking on over the next three years. A few agencies, such as police and fire, also have their own departmental IT plans, but most do not. "If they did them," says IT director Libby Mounts, "it would be far easier for us to put together the automation plan."

After some delay, a new human resources information system is now working. It will provide a great deal more information than the old one, including data for workforce planning.

The city does a good job of making technology training available to its workforce; computer-based IT instruction sits on everyone's desktop. The problem is that many employees don't bother to use it. "They'll tell you they can't train because there's too much going on," says Mounts. "They have more excuses than Carter has pills."

Richmond's Web site is on the weak side, with little financial information.

San Antonio: B-

Technology is well standardized in San Antonio, with the information services department guiding new acquisitions for all the agencies. Automated sharing of information between city departments, as well as between city and county, is routine business here. The police department can perform a "wanted" inquiry, match it against the city's municipal court database, the county's criminal justice database, and state and national criminal databases.

Although San Antonio's financial management and human resource systems are serviceable, managers complain that the systems aren't particularly strong in helping them get at important data. The city is considering upgrading to a fully integrated financial management/human resource system.

Managers complain that making major procurements can be too time-consuming. A big problem is lack of sufficient preparation in the departments, which may go through two or three RFPs before they figure out what they want.

The city is working on its first genuinely strategic IT plan. This much-needed document is due to be completed sometime this year.

San Diego: C

San Diego's managers are still short of the technology they need. Information for personnel management is very weak. There is a sparkling new budget system, but the city's accounting technology is "an old mainframe legacy system that doesn't give a lot of the useful tools that newer systems have," says Richard Wilken, the information technology director. One plus: the budgeting system does provide cost data by activity, a real rarity in the cities.

Departmental IT systems developed here in an inefficient, stove-piped manner. In some areas, such as permitting and engineering, information is not easily accessible across agency boundaries. This will change, however, as San Diego takes likely steps toward an overall IT plan and new IT governance, utilizing a CIO and a steering committee to ensure buy-in from departments.

Twenty years ago, San Diego recognized its problems in attracting and retaining good technical people. So it created the San Diego Data Processing Corp., a city-owned, independent nonprofit corporation that sells IT services, including procurement and maintenance, to the city via an operating agreement. By and large, this experiment has been a success.

San Francisco: C+

San Francisco's IT management is a fragmented affair. The city has a Committee on Information Technology, whose role is to coordinate departmental efforts. But telecommunications is handled separately, under the Department of Technology Information Systems, which also manages many citywide systems dealing with finance and human services. Meanwhile, other large departments, such as the health department, have their own IT units.

The city makes efforts to ensure that new systems are compatible, but "we have gone back and forth on setting standards," says comptroller Ed Harrington. "The last great failure in this regard was selecting Wang as the one and only city standard." A bright spot has been the new HR information system, which supports improved workforce management and hiring. "In some cases, we see approvals in a half an hour that used to take weeks," says Harrington.

CityBusiness, launched in October, is San Francisco's first e-commerce application, allowing businesses to renew tax registrations by credit card. Citizens are encouraged to provide feedback to the city and ask questions via e-mail. The tax collector has committed to responding within one business day.

San Jose: C

San Jose's information technology is relatively weak, especially in the financial area. Budgeting and accounting aren't integrated, so manual intervention is required to make the two systems work together. And financial management isn't integrated with the city's new human resources system.

Although San Jose has made a concerted effort to avoid stovepiped and inconsistent information systems, some departments continue to function autonomously, including streets and traffic, the redevelopment agency, and parks and recreation. Meanwhile, if there's political benefit to an IT investment—for example, if it will benefit a particular council member's district—"we get stuff shoved down our throat," says Jon Walton, deputy director of the information technology department.

The city uses information technology most effectively in capital management, through a system that resides in the public works department. All assets are entered into a database when first created, then repairs over time are logged in. "We track everything that the city maintains or is considered city property," says Walton. "Every tree is tracked by species, age, and when last inspected."

Seattle: B

Seattle's new financial management information system came in $1.5 million under budget and has been generally well received. Its human resources system is also a strength.

There isn't much central control over system development in Seattle, but there is a high level of oversight, and the city has made good progress in improving its strategic planning. Departments can't go off on their own to purchase any significant equipment that hasn't been reviewed. In another effort to make sure it's spending its money effectively, the city has been trying to cut down on an overabundance of contracts. "It's been easy to purchase," says one official, "but not necessarily wisely."

Seattle's Web site is terrific in terms of information offered, but still behind where it should be in allowing citizens to conduct transactions.

Virginia Beach: B

The city has a solid set of standards in place for IT, developed by a Department of Information Technology advisory committee. This committee consists of 40 members, representing most of the city's agencies (including some you wouldn't expect, such as courts).

Managers benefit from relatively strong financial management and capital management information systems. Only human resource technology lags somewhat. "It is basically a payroll system," says David Sullivan. "I wouldn't even call it an HR system." Virginia Beach is now looking into upgrading it.

Some cities have simply taken their senior official assigned to information technology and called him a CIO. Virginia Beach did not do that. "The IT director already had 60 hours' worth of work to do every week," says David Sullivan, who was promoted to the newly created CIO position last summer. "I want to be dealing with strategic issues, not the day-to-day operating issues." A new IT director was brought in for overseeing daily operations, while Sullivan develops the city's first genuinely strategic long-range plan.

Washington, D.C.: C+

Amazing.

A year ago, D.C. government still had 8,000 rotary phones. The city's 541 business locations had no integrated electronic backbone at all. The city was suffering from a decade during which technology was starved for attention.

But signs of progress are all around. For the first time, there are real IT standards and a chief technology officer to manage them. Agencies cannot purchase equipment that's not on the standardized list. The Y2K-remediation process purged many old systems, replacing them with modern technology.

Of course, dramatic IT change can't happen in a nanosecond. Training is still insufficient. Agencies have difficulty transmitting data back and forth. And obsolete data doesn't become useful overnight just because there is new software to move it around.

Appendix C
States

The following text ran in the February 1999 issue of *Governing* magazine, based on reporting done in 1998. The grades listed here were arrived at through a consensus process involving both reporters and editors at *Governing* and academics at the Maxwell School of Citizenship and Public Affairs at Syracuse University. They represent only the grades given in Information Technology— one of the five management areas covered. A handful of states took exception to the text or the evaluation (notably Alaska and Idaho). What's more, given the rapid pace of change in IT, it's unquestionably true that the comments and evaluations would be altered were the write-ups being done today. For example, some months after the report came out, the major outsourcing effort in Connecticut fell through. (See Chapter 9 for more on this subject.) However, for the purpose of this appendix, none of the text has been altered from the original magazine article, as published.

Alabama: D

Alabama appointed its first chief information officer in March 1997. Last September, a new CIO, Eugene Akers, took over the job. "The only way I can go is up," says Akers, who acknowledges that the state has historically done an abysmal job of managing IT.

In his few months of service, Akers has at least lifted the IT process above outright failure level. But he still has an enormous job ahead of him. Major systems provide minimal information to managers, and agencies maintain their own databases of mission-related data. Though Akers wants to move toward standardization, there is no consistent informational architecture. Many agencies historically bought technology to resolve individual problems without planning or project management.

Akers is introducing Alabama to the concept of strategic information technology planning for the first time. He is also forcing agencies to produce business plans before they are allowed to make major purchases.

Alaska: C-

Prior administrations haven't paid much attention to technology in Alaska, and state government is just beginning to move on this front. There is no chief information officer; instead, a Telecommunications Information Council, chaired by the lieutenant governor, serves as the controlling body for IT development and policy standards.

The only IT decisions made centrally are those that require interagency cooperation. Right now, some agencies are riddled with noncompatible systems. Better interoperability, groupware approaches, and integration projects are needed. The state is just moving to its first automated budget information system.

Major improvements have taken place, however, with Alaska's implementation of a wide-area network, which has allowed impressive innovations, such as putting Department of Motor Vehicle functions on-line. The state requires that any agency projects that require communicating with another unit of state government have the capacity to tie in to the network.

While technology specialists are reasonably well trained, IT officials concede that more emphasis needs to be focused on training nontechnical managers in the ways they can use information.

Arizona: D+

"We've got a big hole to dig out of. But we've established the direction for digging out of the hole," says John McDowell, deputy director of

Arizona's Information Technology Agency. All of the state's major systems are woefully out of date, with the exception of the excellent hiring system in human resources. The 1999 legislature will act on a proposal for a new package designed to give both the human resources and financial management agencies an integrated system that will meet more of their current needs.

Up to now, Arizona's telecommunications has been owned and managed on a decentralized basis, with eight or ten different systems for each agency, a prescription for chaos. But the Department of Administration is attempting to set up a single statewide telecommunications system.

Arkansas: D

One state official says it's misleading even to ask about technology systems in Arkansas, because the question "assumes the state has a technology system." As in the case of Managing for Results, Arkansas gets a low grade based on current accomplishments. But if the present state of achievement is weak, there appears to be genuine momentum in this area. The Information Systems Act of 1997 created a new department to centralize IT planning efforts in Arkansas, and a fair number of initiatives appear to be in the early stages of development. The state is preparing policies and standards, and requiring agencies to create individual strategic plans for IT. Perhaps most important, the acting director of the state finance department wrote a letter to the legislature in December requesting funding for a new statewide financial management information system.

California: C+

California established a Department of Information Technology a few years ago. It's headed by a powerful CIO, who reports to the governor and controls the state's $2 billion annual IT budget. Since these changes were made, the state's IT system has made enormous progress.

For the first time, departments are required to create strategic IT

plans, though the state does not do so. While California is not establishing mandated standards, a committee of senior administrative,
procurement and IT professionals is trying to build consensus for
enterprise-wide efforts that will help reduce the number of disparate systems.

The state has master agreements to facilitate procurement of
commodity items. But for major acquisitions, procurement can be
cumbersome, taking a year or so. California is experimenting with
policies that make payment of contracts contingent upon the
proven success of a project. The DOIT also has instituted a risk-
assessment model to follow projects through their life-cycle. As part
of this process, the DOIT has encouraged the proper training and
development of skilled project managers.

For all the improvement, there are considerable problems of fragmentation. Each agency runs its own personnel information system;
some still utilize manual processes. And while the Department of
Finance operates a statewide accounting and budgeting system,
many departments and agencies are on their own in this field as well.

Colorado: C

Colorado has an impressive automated bid system that permits all
procurement opportunities to be posted on the Internet in three
hours and creates solid information to help track data on contracts.
The state has accelerated its request-for-proposal process by cutting
down on the detailed specs included and letting the vendors figure
out solutions to technology problems in their proposals.

Beyond the bidding process, however, IT systems are not integrated. "We have far too many separate systems that by themselves
are doing pretty well," says Andre Pettigrew, executive director of
general support services. "The state is going to have to consider a
fully integrated solution."

Colorado does not have a chief information officer, but it has
created a CIO Forum, which may be a step toward creating a CIO
position and may also lead the way toward overall standardization
of technology.

Connecticut: D+

IT in Connecticut is about to change drastically. The state is currently in the process of outsourcing its entire executive-branch technology effort. "This outsourcing opportunity has been held out as a way to correct some of the deficiencies you see," says Robert Dixon, the state's director of IT planning.

Those deficiencies are considerable. Most agencies do not have computer applications available to assist in program management. Telecommunications is fragmented, hard to manage, and hard to use predictably. Connecticut is behind other states in getting commodity items onto master contracts, and it can take several years to complete the process of procuring major new systems. There are a variety of e-mail systems in place that do not link up with each other very effectively.

On the positive side, the state has started producing IT strategic plans, makes reasonable efforts at training, and is doing a decent if not outstanding job of conveying information via the Internet.

Delaware: B

Delaware is in the process of improving its statewide technology. A new human resources information system is being implemented, although the changeover has taken longer than it should have because a false start cost several months. Among other changes, the state badly needs a new purchasing system to replace one that relies heavily on paper transfers of information. The project was given the go-ahead in December, though some protested that it should wait for resolution of Y2K problems.

The executive director of Delaware's Office of Information Services serves as the state's CIO. The position is cabinet-level and reports directly to the governor. The state's IT planning is very impressive. It includes three-year strategic plans for every agency, followed up six months later by project-oriented budgetary requests. The state rolls the agency plans into an enterprise-wide strategic overlay.

One notable weak point in Delaware's information technology: the state often doesn't effectively justify new IT projects with return on investment or cost-benefit calculations, and it has made little progress in transmitting information to citizens and stakeholders through the Internet.

Florida: C-

The systems and processes with which Florida conducts payroll, human resources, purchasing, accounting and budgeting functions aren't meeting the state's technological needs. They are old, difficult to maintain, and don't provide the kind of management information the government should have. A new integrated human resources system is in the pilot stage, however. Oversight and planning of IT in the state is divided between two groups. One of them, the Technology Review Workgroup, oversees and makes recommendations on agencies' information resource management planning and budgeting proposals.

Unfortunately, its limited staff means that it tends to focus just on big-ticket items (with an eye toward avoiding a repeat of the state's infamous high-tech welfare system that all but blew up almost a decade ago). On the happier side of the floppy disk, the state requires a cost-benefit analysis for any project that exceeds $500,000 in total cost for a year. Its budgeting and appropriations process is available on the Internet, as are performance measures and state audit reports. Florida's Web site captured top honors as the Best State Government Web Site in the country in the second annual Best of the Web competition.

Georgia: C

Georgia does not currently have an integrated information system. But it expects to integrate accounting and personnel data by July of this year, and that should make a big difference. The state is also developing a policy for data warehousing; within the next couple of months, it will be accepting bids for the first phase of a warehouse to help agencies get easier access to information.

Though the state has a CIO, the position's involvement varies depending on the agency. Agencies don't develop IT plans, per se— they create overall strategic plans that give directions and goals, and the IT plan is just an attachment. There is no statewide IT training, and it can be difficult for employees to free up the time to take necessary training.

Historically, Georgia has done little follow-up to see whether results provided by technology investment were commensurate with promises made, outside of the legislative Department of Audits' Performance Management Division. It is attempting to implement such a system now. On the executive side, officials insist, however, that even without the system, they are capable of sensing what works and what does not. "If it were a failure, it would be noticed," says Tom Wagner, director of research and analysis for the Office of Planning and Budget.

Hawaii: F

While other states have been focusing on oversight for information systems, Hawaii has been moving in another direction. The budget for its Information and Communication Services Division is 40 percent lower than it was in 1992. The head of the ICSD has less authority than most other department heads, and no enterprise-wide enforcement of policy procedures, standards or guidelines is possible. "The state procurement office makes rules, but insofar as technology, there are no central rules," says Barbara Tom, planning and project management officer in ICSD.

Competitive bidding is required for any technology purchase over $25,000. Often, says Tom, "by the time we get the bid out, it's obsolete." Now, the governor has mandated that he wants to approve all technology purchases that amount to $10,000 or more.

Hawaii does require all departments to prepare and update annual plans for IT, and it asks for a cost-benefit analysis of new projects. But since there's little or no review of either effort, they're pretty much just paper exercises.

Idaho: D+

There is no chief information officer in Idaho, although there is a centralized agency, the Information Technology Resource Management Council, which sets policy and standards for IT. Standardization is slowly coming, but completion of consistent rules is still a year away.

Meanwhile, agencies have started to prepare strategic information technology plans, but there are huge gaps in the capacity to do that effectively. The centralized human resources technology maintained by the state provides little information that is useful to agency managers. It cannot produce reports that are customized to their needs. In terms of the state's centralized accounting systems, there are ways that agencies can access useful information, but the process required to do so can be laborious and time-consuming.

In general, Idaho agencies find sharing information to be a difficult chore. Sending e-mail can require a phone call first to get the e-mail address. "You have people with databases that are five or ten years old," says one information technology official, "and just sharing information is problematic. Or they're not trained. Or they'll send you something and you'll run it on your database program and it doesn't work."

Illinois: D+

Information technology has not yet become a management tool for budgeting at the agency level. The state does maintain a centralized accounting system, but about a quarter of the state's executive branch agencies—including some of the very largest ones—have thus far elected not to use it.

The technology used in the personnel system, meanwhile, is old and needs replacement. Actually, there are three personnel systems—for benefits, payroll and other human resource activities. They tie into one another, however.

Illinois is one of only a handful of states that doesn't have a department designated to the information technology function. The closest it comes is a bureau within the Department of Central Management Services. No surprise, then, that there's not a great deal of standardization beyond the requirement that new developments fit into the single state network. There is, however, a five-year strategic IT plan, updated each year, which leads the agencies in the creation of their annual IT plans.

Procurement of major projects is somewhat slow, and the state doesn't require much in the way of return-on-investment or cost-benefit analysis outside of major outsourcing projects.

Indiana: C

Indiana's budgeting still relies on old-fashioned calculations, processes and controls. The state plans on developing a new procedure, but such efforts are still in early stages. Meanwhile, new personnel and procurement systems will begin providing far more in the way of useful management information later this year.

There's minimal inter-agency use of data right now, a problem the state plans on tackling. But solutions may be hard to find as long as there is no statewide strategic IT plan.

On the positive side, the Access Indiana Information Network is one of the most comprehensive citizen transaction networks in the U.S. Not only are Hoosiers able to view some 70,000 pages of government information on-line, but the program doesn't cost taxpayers a penny. Vendors are given access to commercially viable data, such as drivers' records, then sell it and reimburse the state. Everyone wins under this plan.

Iowa: C+

The enterprise-wide information systems the state has been working with have not supported management effectively. "If the new governor asks how many employees we have, it can take several dozen people to get the answer," says Tom Shepherd, administrator for business and finance.

But in June, the state will begin full implementation of the Iowa Financial Accounting System, which will provide direct interfaces with a brand-new human resources system and should provide managers with tons of on-line data, allowing procurement policy, for example, to be enforced electronically.

The state is justifiably proud that it owns its own fiber-optics network. It is just beginning to eliminate segregated silos of information by putting together data warehouses. Efforts are underway to define more specific technology standards, as well as to develop a comprehensive system for measuring the effectiveness of IT in general.

Kansas: C+

Each Kansas agency has its own budget information system; the data from these individual systems is keyed into a central system. This antique accounting procedure produces little useful information. It's due for replacement in three years, but if the state decides to follow the rest of the nation and adopts GAAP accounting, the informational transition can't begin until the books are converted.

Kansas' IT policies are in a state of metamorphosis generally. New legislation has created a position of chief state information architect, a high-level policy committee to develop the IT architecture itself, and IT officer positions for all three branches of government. Detailed cost-benefit analysis is being conducted for all new projects. A new statewide training program will be keyed to the architecture that's being developed; the state will pay bonuses to employees who develop necessary skills.

Though the state makes most commodity items available through master contracts, procurement of larger, more complex systems is overly time-consuming.

Kentucky: C+

Kentucky has recently instituted a solid multiyear technology planning process. It has a dedicated $175 million technology trust fund, to be used for projects that can reimburse the fund through clear monetary savings.

The state's accounting and purchasing information systems aren't yet integrated. Many agencies use their own, and while some systems are electronic, purchasing is still a manual process in many cases. Agency managers can make speedy purchases of commodity items through state-negotiated contracts, but larger projects require line-item approval by the General Assembly, and easily get ensnared in a cumbersome procurement process that can take eight months or more.

The Empower Kentucky reengineering initiatives will make an enormous difference in IT. Many future technology efforts will be required to promise cost benefits, and cabinet secretaries will be asked to sign a commitment to deliver those savings. The only real problem is that projects not connected with an Empower Kentucky initiative are under no such obligation.

Louisiana: C-

Louisiana suffers from the drawbacks of deeply decentralized, unplanned IT, with unintegrated, unstandardized systems slowing many processes. A modern budgeting system is needed and is in development.

There is a great deal of momentum in other information areas. A new financial accounting system went on-line last May, and by next year, a new human resources system will be in place. A chief information officer will be appointed by the governor sometime in 1999, and will report to the commissioner of administration.

Louisiana has far too many databases and is trying to coordinate them, beginning with an inventory project that started last summer. It seems to have gone overboard in negotiating master contacts with too many vendors: it now has more than 60 individual brand-name contracts. This "takes up a great deal of time with only one person to handle the process," a state official complains.

Maine: C

IT systems for budgeting in Maine fall far short of the state's needs, and are little help to agencies in developing their budgets or to the budget bureau in solving its analytical problems. Hopes for a new information system were stalled in the legislature in the midst of a debate over whether or not the new system should support performance budgeting.

The state maintains a data warehouse, which provides agencies with easy access to central personnel and financial information, and funds are available for ongoing modernization of a wide-area network. A strong central office oversees technology use, but Maine lacks central monitoring of projects as they move from development to implementation; new proposed legislation may help alleviate that. In an effort to encourage employees to become better trained in technology, the state is giving a 5 percent salary stipend to individuals who get 40 hours of training during the course of the year.

Maryland: C

The information provided by Maryland's accounting system isn't sufficient for individual agencies; many build their own as a result. There is no statewide human resources information system. When the state went through collective bargaining recently, and unions asked for data, it was a time-consuming task to pry it out. However, the state is designing a comprehensive, on-line budget-preparation system.

There's little standardization here outside of mainframes. Even e-mail uses different software, making message-sending a sometimes frustrating effort. Though the Office of Information Technology manages all telecommunications, voice and data transmissions are managed as separate entities.

Major acquisitions follow standard, cumbersome, and time-consuming procurement laws.

On the positive side, the state has relatively strong training efforts; it pushes agencies to make sure that they provide ample instruction. The state's fast-moving efforts at managing for results are likely to be helpful in identifying the actual benefits of technology systems. And Maryland does a reasonably good job of sharing information with its citizens over the Internet.

Massachusetts: C

Information management is a mixed bag in Massachusetts—the accounting and budgeting systems feature an integrated database of information that's easily available to managers, while the statewide personnel system can't generate useful data. Many of the state's agencies run stand-alone systems that would benefit from consolidation. There are a couple of dozen different systems related to the state's welfare business alone.

Massachusetts has a decentralized telecommunications system, and although logic would dictate some form of unification, the will to bring that about has been missing. "There's a huge amount of parochialism and a real desire not to give it up," says David Lewis, acting IT director.

Generally, the state's IT procurement efforts are good, with one interesting innovation: every spring, the state holds something called the "Big Buy." All agencies with money to buy PCs do so at that time, rather than returning the money to the general fund. This enables the state to make a massive one-time purchase, and get costs down to the bone. Most funding for major IT systems in Massachusetts has been accomplished through bonds—which requires a reasonably high level of scrutiny, including cost-benefit analyses.

Michigan: B+

Michigan maintains excellent centralized accounting, purchasing, budgeting and human resource information systems—as well as a centralized management database from which information can be easily extracted for analysis and reporting.

Agencies maintain some top-notch mission-specific systems as well. For example, the Office of Retirement Systems is supported by mainframes that provide on-line data to customer service reps, who then respond to retiree questions.

The state has consolidated all its data centers, as well as its telecommunications networks, resulting in significant savings. Its staff is well trained in technology use, and there is an excellent procurement system.

The one real weakness here is the absence of a statewide strategic plan (other than for the Y2K problem) that would guide information technology planning on a long-term basis. That weakness may soon be remedied. Michigan is also struggling to get a fix on ways of evaluating the returns it is getting from technology projects.

Minnesota: B

Minnesota maintains reasonably up-to-date centralized information systems, which deposit a great variety of useful data into warehouses set up to allow trained managers to manipulate it. Budgeting is done through a comprehensive statewide system used by all agencies and the legislature, providing a common background for its development and analysis.

Minnesota's chief information officer reports directly to the governor. Minnesota has compiled its second statewide master plan for technology. The first was largely a visionary document, according to an Office of Technology official. But the state has now integrated this strategic approach with its real-world technology efforts.

One major obstacle in IT here is the lengthy procurement process for major acquisitions. It can take more than half a year to acquire a large system, though reform has begun. Meanwhile, the state is grappling with the challenge of requiring agencies to justify their acquisitions with cost-benefit analysis.

Minnesota's Web site points users to a wide variety of state government information resources. There is one potential stumbling block, however: a Minnesota law stating that data cannot be used for other purposes than those for which it was collected. This hasn't been much of a problem yet, but it likely will be as use of the Internet grows.

Mississippi: C-

Mississippi's automated accounting system doesn't provide much in the way of reports or useful information for managers. However, there is a data warehouse from which information can be easily accessed. The state's new human resources system was designed to export data to the warehouse.

Centralized IT management in the state concerns itself primarily with statewide systems such as the data center and a backbone network that provides video support. There is no standardization of nonmainframe software and almost no agency oversight. Mississippi doesn't have an integrated e-mail system, although many staffers do have access to the Internet. There's no central control over IT training, and when the state does offer classes, they are often under-enrolled.

Agency plans for information technology go out three years. They are reviewed mostly just to make sure they conform to the budget. The statewide plan contains very little realistic planning beyond one year.

The process of procuring major assets in the information field can take up to eight or ten months; if vendors protest, that can add another three to six months.

Missouri: B+

Missouri's technology acquisition process has won several prestigious awards. It features a "prime vendor" system: the state arranges with a single vendor to offer virtually every needed commodity item at 6 percent over acquisition price. The state probably could have negotiated down to 4 percent, but wanted guarantees that the vendor would provide top-notch service, as assessed through customer satisfaction surveys and performance measures.

Primary systems, while functional, fall short on providing specialized information to managers. To call the HR system an information system "would be to flatter it," says one manager. But next July, Missouri will roll out the first stage of a new, completely integrated accounting, budgeting, purchasing and human resources system that should make access to data a stroll in the cyber-park. It is scheduled for complete implementation in about two and a half years.

Missouri has a centralized management structure, in which the CIO reports directly to the governor, controls budgets and is responsible for IT standards and planning. Agencies as well as the state plan out three years ahead. The state is in the first stages of measuring the effectiveness of its IT systems from a central perspective.

Montana: B-

Montana is engaged in one of the biggest IT upgrades around, with the so-called Montana Prime, a comprehensive and integrated financial, human resources and budgeting system. On April 1, the HR component will come on-line, and the financial piece will be implemented on July 1. "Now we can dream up and craft a report in a day or two that would have taken months before," says Tony Herbert, administrator of the information services division.

Standardization is important and widespread in the state. Agencies publish plans that are fundamentally project-oriented, not very strategic, but are eventually rolled up into a statewide plan, with a more potent strategic overlay.

The process of purchasing large systems is cumbersome and time-consuming; it goes through the state's standard procurement procedures, which are not appropriate for fast-moving IT. Training is not a strong point, and many IT professionals have to fly out of state to keep up to date. For end users, "typically, they don't want to get training," says Herbert, "and they don't have the budgets anyhow. So it doesn't happen."

Nebraska: C+

The biggest problem with Nebraska information technology is its human resources system. The system tells virtually nothing about state employees other than their official leave status. State leaders have been advised to implement a fully integrated information system, including human resources, accounting, purchasing, and budgeting, but in a state known for fiscal caution, don't bet on its chances.

Meanwhile, the state has just acquired, free of charge from South Dakota, the application framework for a budgeting system developed to permit some scenario-building for budgeters. Unfortunately, it isn't integrated into other systems.

Nebraska hasn't made much of an effort to standardize IT procurements, though it has operated a single mainframe data center for some 31 years (upgrading technology over time, of course), in order to avoid the costs associated with the proliferation of multiple single-purpose computing environments.

Though agencies are required to submit an Information Management and Technology Plan that extends through the biennium and beyond, the state itself has no strategic IT plan. That may change, however, with the arrival of its first chief information officer. The state does an excellent job at sharing information electronically, statewide.

Nevada: C

Nevada has new or revamped systems on-line or in the works for nearly every category of information. The biggest item is a newly introduced integrated financial system that links accounting, budgeting, personnel, payroll, and purchasing. The state is also working on major systems for its Department of Motor Vehicles and the child/family program. It's upgrading Medicaid technology and is developing a revenue reporting system for the department of taxation. Finally, it's in the process of enhancing its statewide network.

"We were so far behind, we recognized the need to aggressively move in the technology area," says IT director Marlene Lockard. "In some areas, they've been working with a number two pencil and a legal pad." Nevada has just developed a five-year strategic IT plan, and Lockard's position, already given cabinet-level status, is getting more legislative support.

Though many statewide information standards are in place, a handful of large agencies don't fall under central control. The Department of Transportation has its own data center and is exempt from any central planning. Why? That's the way it has always been.

Some other areas are in need of improvement as well. The procurement process is slow and paper-intensive, and the state is still deficient in training funds, though the IT office is aggressively going after more money for that effort.

New Hampshire: C

New Hampshire has a comprehensive integrated financial management and human resources information system. It meets ongoing needs but is not useful for providing customized reports that managers would like. The state is focusing on making the current system Y2K-compliant before it looks at replacements.

Most agencies cannot use data systems (or even e-mail) to communicate with each other. However, a State Unified Network is being designed to connect them within the next year.

In a state with little strategic planning of any sort, the fact that IT is beginning to have a formal planning process is impressive. However, it's a new effort, and the plans developed by agencies thus far are mostly lists of desired procurements, with little in the way of strategy. One positive note: the state is trying to incorporate more knowledge of technology in its management training; so even managers who aren't directly involved in IT will have a better idea how to use it in their programs.

New Hampshire's chief information officer originally reported to the governor, but that raised concern that the position risked becoming politicized; the CIO now reports to the commissioner of administrative services.

New Jersey: B-

New Jersey uses statewide standards in telecommunications, and its Garden State Network provides a telecommunications architecture. It is moving toward standardization of other systems as well. Mainframes in particular have gone through a period of consolidation recently. The state's centralized systems generally are good information management tools, with the prominent exception of human resources, which features a 30-year old payroll component.

The state has no enterprise-wide strategic plan, but creating one is a goal of the newly appointed CIO, who has put together strategic planning teams.

The Office of Information Technology doesn't require strict return on investments for new projects—though the budget office would like those kinds of figures—but it is moving toward developing a means for evaluating IT efforts.

New Mexico: C

New Mexico's first chief information officer came on board in September of 1996. "There was no staff, no office, nothing," says CIO

Jim Hall. Since then, standards have been put into place for personal computers, software applications and other technology, and the standardization process is moving forward.

The state still has a long way to go. Major IT systems offer a reasonable amount of operational support, but the systems are all free-standing and don't support cross-functional analysis. Meanwhile, about half the agencies run their own networks, which makes data-sharing very difficult.

The CIO's power in New Mexico emanates largely from his impact on the planning process. "I have a lot of influence over who gets what money," Hall says. Each agency prepares a technology plan with guidance from the CIO's office, which then reviews all procurements in light of this work.

New Mexico has just completed its first statewide information technology plan, which is much more strategic in nature than those produced by the agencies.

New York: C

New York created an Office for Technology in 1997. Its director serves as the state's chief information officer and reports to the director of state operations. The OFT is enacting "preferred standards," which agencies are expected to adopt over time as their systems change or they make major modifications. New York is developing a new human resources information system, too, which will help.

Meanwhile, however, the state has numerous independent systems for financial management, human resources and capital management, and they use a bewildering variety of platforms, software and data formats. Telecommunications and data communications are not integrated throughout the state, though the OFT is coordinating a project to create a statewide Intranet that will support data voice and video for state and local government. OFT also is beginning a multiyear project to consolidate 24 data centers.

On the positive side, training for IT professionals in all agencies is provided as part of a statewide plan in New York, and the state is well known for the quality of its technology workforce. There's some use of cost benefits in the RFP process.

North Carolina: C

Curiously, North Carolina doesn't know exactly how much it spends on IT. That's because many agencies are run by independently elected officials, who haven't been interested in sharing information with a centralized agency or cooperating in the state's planning process.

The state is now altering its planning approach to one that encourages agencies to put together a technology "portfolio" of assets that contribute to their work.

The state's chief information officer reports to the Commerce Department. This seems odd, but it may buffer him from the political difficulties of reporting to a constitutionally weak governor.

The information available to North Carolina's accounting process is great. However, four separate systems that deal with personnel are old and unintegrated with each other or with the accounting system. Dealing with more than one system—required for something as simple as hiring someone—is an arduous task.

Large procurements in North Carolina go through a cumbersome, time-consuming process. But the state is working on procurement reform.

North Dakota: B-

North Dakota's budget passes through both the executive and legislative branches without ever needing a paper document. There is a centralized accounting and management information system, and it is on-line in real time for all agencies. But the personnel information system does not provide centralized information for agencies. Each agency is responsible for much of its own personnel data.

North Dakota currently has a chief information officer, appointed by the state director of OMB; legislation is being introduced to have the CIO report directly to the governor.

The state is heading in the right direction in a variety of ways. Its Information Services Division recently completed the first statewide technology plan and has been given authority to exercise oversight on the agencies. Multiyear technology planning has begun.

Agencies have been asked to provide a cost-benefit analysis for new projects. The first round of such efforts produced some information, and the project is moving forward.

And although the state is only now embarking on an effort to produce formal IT standards, many agencies have been following de facto standards. Even absent a powerful central authority, North Dakota hasn't had many problems with fragmentation. A small state, it has just one data center, one agency out of which operational services work, one network. The state Web site is excellent.

Ohio: B

Ohio is upgrading its statewide accounting information system, which will include a reporting database component and will allow agencies to customize their own reports. A new human resources system began implementation last spring, allowing for efficient use of significant data.

One of the biggest efforts on the IT front is the development of a full conceptual architecture for technology. Committees, staffed from the agencies, are developing standards and guidelines. The process will be completed next June.

Ohio has an award-winning digital fiber-optic communication infrastructure already in place. It serves public television and radio, public libraries, schools, colleges and universities, and some state agencies. Total cost: about $107 million. Savings over the previous system: about $12 million a year.

The state's e-mail systems aren't as effective as they should be, and communication can be troublesome. In addition, agencies are frustrated with the time required to satisfy the state's procurement people with the detail in RFPs. A complicated RFP can take a year to complete.

Oklahoma: C-

Oklahoma operates an integrated network, called OneNet, which connects schools, courts, libraries, hospitals, and state, local and federal agencies across the state. Outside of OneNet, however, there is not a great deal of standardization in Oklahoma's IT systems. Agencies tend to migrate on their own to relatively consistent industry-driven protocols, but there are odd exceptions: not long ago, the Oklahoma Senate decided to purchase an Apple-based system, while virtually everyone else in state government uses IBM-compatibles.

Oklahoma's centralized accounting information system has a great deal of capacity to be used for agency management. But most managers don't take advantage of the opportunity. The personnel information system is utilized to a greater extent.

The state has no chief information officer, though the director of information services in the office of state finance serves in a similar role. There is no statewide IT plan; all agencies submit separate plans that tend to focus on procurement.

Oregon: C+

Oregon's new CIO has moved a technologically laggard state forward rapidly. A five-year IT policy plan has been approved, taking in all branches of government and localities as well. The state controller has done a multibranch business process analysis to explore areas that technology ought to support better or differently. The state's obsolete budget information system, originally scheduled for replacement in the 2001–2003 cycle, is now supposed to be completed in the next biennium.

Oregon avoids specific IT standards, preferring to work toward an open architecture in which information technology is interoperable. However, the state has not yet achieved that vision. For all the emphasis on performance measurement, managers can't easily search for performance information across agencies. The database that would allow that is still in the process of development.

Pennsylvania: B

As part of a new effort, agencies perform cost-benefit analysis and draw up performance measures each year for proposed IT projects that run over $20,000. The following year, the projects are audited to see if the benefits are being delivered. "If you don't perform," the state warns, "you may not receive money in subsequent years' requests."

There is no classic strategic plan for Pennsylvania information technology, though agencies develop independent plans with the help of the central office. The state does mandate specific goals, however. This year, every agency is required to develop two commerce-based electronic applications. The state also is developing a so-called "on-line shopping cart," which will allow agencies to see what vendors have to offer, order right from their desktops and ultimately have their accounts debited.

Pennsylvania has received national recognition for its Link to Learn initiative, using information technology as a catalyst for improving education at all levels. Concern about IT and the schools has led the state to spend $2.3 million to make sure schools are Y2K-compliant—possibly the only state to launch such an extensive effort in this area.

Rhode Island: D

"Giant strides have been taken," Rhode Island says of its IT operations, "but they have just gotten us to the starting line." Absolutely true. The state's central computer systems are Stone Age, providing little information to managers. The state has recently completed a contract to build a new financial management information system, which will begin to roll out over the next few months.

Rhode Island has just begun an overall planning process for IT. The state allows agencies to buy many commodity-type items from a master list, but for more complex purchases the process is numbingly difficult. Approvals travel from desk to desk, and can take inordinate amounts of time to be completed. It can easily take two or three years to purchase a major system. Finally, the state has little clue as to whether its purchases are paying off. "We don't have any way of knowing cost benefits or return on investment," says one IT official. "We're still trying to figure out what the costs are."

In 1996, the state appointed a chief information officer and has begun to consider an effort to standardize its IT systems, which are currently very decentralized.

South Carolina: B

South Carolina put in a new human resources information system in 1997 and has also implemented new procurement technology. The state's accounting system needs replacement, though; many agencies have had to design their own to make up for its poor quality. The comptroller general has asked the general assembly for funds for a new statewide system.

South Carolina has a reasonably fast procurement schedule for IT. It is moving toward a coordinated training approach, and is developing a core curriculum for IT professionals to use as a model.

There is no chief information officer; planning and oversight of IT are divided among three separate offices. The state also has an unwieldy collection of 11 different data centers; a state controller's report has recommended that they be consolidated into one by July 2001, and estimated that this would save the state $30 million over ten years.

South Carolina does a good job of sharing information with citizens. Rather than just sending agencies out to set up Web sites in a helter-skelter fashion, it did a survey to determine what kind of information its citizens wanted on the Internet. The first thing they wanted? Job leads.

South Dakota: B

As with human resources, South Dakota has a very centralized IT system. The chief information officer oversees everything from desktop computers to telecommunications. All technology is either standardized or developed by the CIO's staff.

Unfortunately, the state's central systems are not well integrated, and users who want to employ data for managing sometimes have to go to several different systems for helpful information.

South Dakota does have a strategic plan for information technology. Only a handful of agencies have written their own plans, but the CIO is trying to push them in that direction and their absence may be less of a problem here than in decentralized states.

The acquisitions process is reasonably speedy, and all large acquisitions are done centrally. The state does a cost-benefit analysis on major projects. Generally—though not always—there's a follow-up.

Though the state does an acceptable job of offering IT training, agencies don't always go along. They balked, for example, when the CIO demanded a half-day of training for all agency employees on the state's desktop operating system. "I can't tell you how many agencies tried to talk me out of it," he says. "We forced it on them. You go to some agencies and their people are starved for knowing what to do."

Tennessee: B+

Tennessee's IT system is highly standardized, under a powerful CIO who is unafraid to pull the plug on floundering projects. "The biggest mistake is to chase a bad project down a hole," he says. The state has a comprehensive information planning process involving all the major institutional players; agencies prepare their own plans covering three years. Technology training is increasingly strong, with an average of between one and two weeks of training for every technical worker in the state.

The state's centralized information systems have not been doing a particularly good job of producing the data to track state government performance, but they should do better with the help of new data warehouses that will make more information available to managers.

Much of Tennessee's capital IT funding is offered as loans to agencies; this holds them accountable for a project's promised return on investment, because agency managers are held accountable for repaying the loans.

Texas: B

Though Texas has attempted to develop statewide information management in the financial and human resources areas, most agencies use their own internal information systems for management processes. The state does, however, use a statewide budgeting system that supports both the executive and legislative budget offices, and even tracks performance measures.

Texas has only minimal IT standards, but it encourages agencies to make acquisitions that are interoperable with those in other agencies. There is a five-year strategic IT plan. Agencies also produce five-year IT plans, listing goals and objectives, and the state reviews them to make sure they are aligned with the statewide direction.

The Department of Information Resources brokers purchases of commodity hardware, software and even information services. In 1998, this saved agencies a reported $30 million on such purchases through the power of quantity buying.

Although the agencies control most of their own technology, the DIR does monitor the largest among them—right now, about 25 separate efforts. It does a so-called "post-implementation evaluation review," in which it forces agencies to compare the qualitative and quantitative benefits promised at the beginning of projects to the ultimate success in delivering them.

Utah: B+

A statewide data warehouse provides financial, human resources and payroll information in Utah over a wide-area network. It allows users to generate their own reports at any time, saving the state more than $5 million annually in report development costs. The state's personnel management system is top-notch.

Utah's IT planning process is thorough and complete and has attracted national attention. This year, the IT office was moved to the cabinet level. The state also is in the early stages of formally designating architecture and standards. Although many de facto standards exist, "we need improvement in terms of making it written," says chief information officer David Moon. Moon also believes that individual agencies need to provide more time for employee training in information technology, and that the state needs more central coordination of training opportunities. At the moment, with training provided on an agency-by-agency basis, the state misses out on economies of scale.

Vermont: C

The information provided by Vermont's budget and accounting systems is inadequate. It doesn't even properly support the long-awaited conversion to generally accepted accounting principles. Vermont has requested vendor proposals for a new system that will include budgeting, accounting and purchasing modules, but it won't be in place until 2001.

The state's information office used to be a one-person operation. Now it is a two-person operation: the CIO has a lone assistant, working full-time on the Year 2000 problem. The CIO does, however, write a five-year plan for the state's information technology needs, chair an advisory commission, approve all requests for proposal, recommend decisions on IT contracts and manage statewide network infrastructure. Whew!

Agencies help out (a little) by providing five-year IT plans. They are required to include cost-benefit analysis of all projects in excess of $150,000, though there's no follow-through, at least so far.

On the bright side, the state has a robust shared network infrastructure that eases communication among agencies and branches of government. More than 300 of the state's 350 schools are able to make use of the system, and citizens can go to any public library for access to government information as well as other Web sites.

Virginia: A-

Virginia's centralized IT systems provide a great deal of information for its managers. The state is moving toward a total integration of systems to make the data available more quickly and easily.

There is no off-the-shelf software that will fully integrate the performance-based budgeting process with the accounting process, so Virginia is working to create its own. A new human resources system is coming on-line as well.

The IT effort is centrally coordinated by a powerful chief information officer who not only oversees the internal management efforts but also works to attract new technology businesses to the state.

Strategic information planning is top-notch, with solid coordination between statewide plans and agency plans. A huge array of information is easily accessible to citizens through the state's Web site.

Technology training could be better. The acquisition process leaves something to be desired, too, with large, complex procurements taking six months or more. Part of the problem is that IT purchases are governed by the Virginia Public Procurement Act—a statute not designed for the fast-moving high-tech world.

Washington: A

Washington is an innovator in this category. Its new centralized Performance Measure Tracking System allows agencies to enter and monitor progress against their own standards, a relative rarity in the states. The state data warehouse project was named on a list of the "most innovative computing projects in American business."

The Department of Information Services markets its services in competition with the private sector. If the services it is providing aren't in demand—as happened, for example, with maintenance for desktop computers—it shuts them down, just like a business would.

At the moment, Washington is changing its information planning process from one that dealt with individual projects—going through the usual route of budget submission, legislative approval and implementation—to a new process called "portfolio management." The idea here is that agencies maintain a portfolio of technology in the same way an investor might have a portfolio of stock. New investments must fit into the overall portfolio, not merely solve a single problem. This should be phased in statewide within a year.

Generally, the state doesn't fund an IT project for more than two years. For the big ones, it appropriates enough money to get Phase I completed, and then demands results before moving on.

West Virginia: C

The state has reasonable management of its information technology, with a chief technology officer reporting directly to the governor, as well as centralized efforts to set policies and standards. West Virginia does a good job at training IT workers with limited resources. It even has a pretty good four-year enterprise-wide Information Technology Plan.

Still, too many sensible plans wind up buried in a pile of dead dreams. "I just came from a budget hearing," Sam Tully, the chief technology officer, reported recently. "That's when the administration determines we don't have enough money to fund these things. So, we do it with less, or don't do it, or let it wait a year."

Though the state plans to get a better human resources information system, that process has been delayed. Two agencies are actively pursuing data warehouses, but there's no assurance right now that either will get funding.

Meanwhile, procurement policies designed to avoid corruption also can make any sizable purchase into a nightmare of red tape. Legislation in this state holds individuals personally responsible for any purchasing foul-ups. This inclines managers to drag as many people into the approval process as possible. "Hell," says one observer, "you're putting your house on the line."

Wisconsin: B

The IT planning process here is top-notch, with planning done statewide, at the agency level and by individual organizations within agencies. Wisconsin is ahead of the pack in requiring agencies to use a standard cost-benefit methodology in making funding requests. It also is one of the national leaders in IT training, which is made affordable to agencies through centralized funding.

Although the state has no chief information officer, it does have an effectively standardized IT system, from mainframes to desktops. Network-level telecommunications are largely integrated.

Even so, there are problems. The budget information system is old and can't really handle its job; human resources has no central system at all; the accounting information system is better, but its ability to generate reports is far from state of the art. Wisconsin plans to remedy this by gathering a wide array of information into a data warehouse. This should help the situation a great deal.

Wyoming: D+

A couple of years ago, Wyoming's central information technology department turned over a number of its top people to the individual state agencies in a decentralization effort. Since the IT department is funded largely by billing the agencies—and these people were some of its top billers—this move effectively crippled the functioning of the central office.

The state does have a chief information officer, but he is responsible for strategic planning, not information technology planning. Though the position may be strengthened, right now the agencies control their own agendas.

Most of Wyoming's information systems are functional but provide little useful data to make broad-based management decisions. There is no data warehouse. The personnel information system is about to be replaced, and the new one should facilitate management in that area.

The state does a reasonably good job at procuring new technology. However, training is not strong, and money is wasted because there's so little central coordination among agencies. While the agencies are required to do a cost-benefit analysis for new procurements, they are not held accountable for their decisions after the purchases are made.

Appendix D
Glossary

Application—A piece of software created to perform a specific function; for example, spreadsheet analysis.

Architecture—The overall set of standards in place in a city or state.

Business case—One of a variety of ways to demonstrate the value of an IT procurement. Ideally, a business case demonstrates the ways in which the purchase will serve to improve services or save money for the city or state.

CD-ROM—Short for compact disc, read-only memory. A type of storage media for data; it can contain many times the amount of information of a standard floppy disc.

Chief information officer—Often called a CIO, this is generally the most senior position directly responsible for information technology in a city or state government. The amount of authority the CIO has varies from entity to entity, as does the specific nature of the job description.

Client/server—Used on a network, clients are the computers that use information provided by another computer called a server.

Commodity technology—Purchases that are made in large quantities by a city or state, for example, personal computers. Generally, individual RFPs do not have to be created for commodity items. Increasingly, they are purchased through master contracts.

Compatible—Two pieces of information technology that can work together, sharing data or tasks, are said to be compatible.

Cost-benefit analysis—The effort to compare the cost of a proposed purchase with the potential benefits (both monetary and non-monetary), with an eye toward making sure it's a worthwhile investment.

Decentralization—The process of giving more power and authority over procurement and implementation of information technology to agencies.

Distance learning—Any of a variety of ways in which computers can be used to educate, with the source of information coming from a central source and the recipients spread over a geographically wide area.

Distributed system—A computer system that can be accessed by multiple users.

End-users—The people who actually use technology in cities or states. End-users can range from high-level managers who use budgeting software to clerical workers who may only use word processing.

GIS—Stands for Geographic Information Systems, a very popular kind of software that permits cities and states to overlay enormous quantities of data on a geographic basis. In this way, for example, a manager could correlate the percentage of people living in poverty in a certain county with the average income in that county, and the absentee rate in schools there.

GPP—Stands for the Government Performance Project, an effort, funded by the Pew Charitable Trusts, to evaluate how well cities, states, and counties are managed in five areas: Information Technology, Financial Management, Capital Management. Human Resources, and Managing for Results. Partners in the GPP have been *Governing* magazine and the Maxwell School at Syracuse University, and results are published annually in *Governing*. Most of the information for this book was drawn from the GPP.

GUI—Pronounced "gooey," it stands for graphical user interface. It means any of a variety of means by which computers can present information graphically—using icons, or menus, for example—to ease access for users.

Hacker—An individual who intrudes into computer systems to which he or she is not ordinarily granted access. Sometimes the goal is to get information; in malicious instances, a hacker may alter something within the computer.

Hit—On the Internet a single visit to a Web site is called a hit.

Imaging—Creating digital copies of documents for easy electronic storage.

Intranet—A network that exists within a city or a state and can be accessed only by users within that entity, or others who are permitted.

Legacy system—A computer system that is still in use in a city or a state, dating from a time prior to the installation of a newer generation of technology.

Low bid—The process by which one criteria (and sometimes the only criteria) for a purchase is that it is the least expensive available product to fit previously outlined criteria.

Mainframe computer—Generally a very powerful computer, capable of the most intensive tasks. At one time, most functions in cities and states were performed by mainframes. However, they have been replaced in many instances by desktop computers, and by client/server systems.

Master contracts—Also called blanket contracts, these are arrangements in which a city or state contracts for goods or services with a preapproved set of vendors. If money is available, agencies can then purchase from the list of vendors who are under master contracts without need for a complex procurement process.

Modem—The piece of technology that allows a computer to communicate with other computers via phone lines, cable lines, or other media.

Network—Computers that can easily communicate with one another because they are connected through common communications technology.

Outsourcing—Using private sector corporations to perform tasks that otherwise would be done by employees working directly for a government. For example, if a city decided that it didn't want to be responsible for servicing its own desktop computers, it might outsource that operation to a company that specialized in this work.

Performance measures—Means for determining how efficiently and effectively government investments are functioning. Generally they are divided into three categories: inputs (the amount of money spent), outputs (the actual work delivered, for example, the number of measles inoculations given), and outcomes (the actual results of the investment, for example, the decline or rise in the number of cases of measles as a result of an inoculation program).

Redundant systems—Information technology systems that essentially perform the same job. For example, if three agencies all had imaging systems that could easily be replaced by one, more efficient, entity-wide system, all three would be redundant.

Request for proposal (RFP)—The document that spells out the details for a proposed purchase and is used by vendors to actually write their proposals, in hopes of making a sale.

Search engine—A type of programming that allows a user to submit a term or group of terms—usually on a Web site—and discover where they are found.

Shadow systems—When a government establishes an entity-wide system, but individual agencies establish their own in order to augment the entity-wide capacities for their own use, these additional ones are called "shadow systems."

Stakeholder—Anyone who is the beneficiary of a government service, or who is involved in the process of providing these services, including, but not limited to, citizens, corporate taxpayers, and legislative and executive branch employees—both elected and appointed.

Standardization—The effort to ensure that information technology systems are compatible, and that they are technologically capable of sharing data effectively and easily.

Stovepipe system—An information technology system that is not compatible with many others in a city or a state. A stovepipe system has often been purchased or built by an agency without regard to the nature of systems operating elsewhere in the same entity.

Strategic planning—The effort to think about the future of a government's information technology in a way that ties a vision for the city or state to goals and objectives (that should be measurable) and ultimately to the procurement and implementation of new IT systems.

Tactical plan—As distinct from a strategic plan, a document that shows future planned procurements for information technology; it generally does not tie these very specific decisions in with broader visions and objectives (see Strategic planning).

Webmaster—The individual who is responsible for technologically maintaining a Web site.

Web site—A collection of information and graphics that can be reached with a computer and a modem on the World Wide Web. City and state Web sites can be used not only to provide information, but also to allow citizens to communicate with and conduct transactions with the government.

Y2K bug—Now ancient history, it represented the Year 2000 bug, which many feared would cause many computers in cities and states to crash. Its root was in the failure of programmers to anticipate that by using two digit dates, computers wouldn't be able to distinguish, for example, between 2001 and 1901.

Index